T
HANDBOOK

BRIAN PERREN

Capital Transport

C O N T E N T S

Second Edition
ISBN 185414 195 3
Published by Capital Transport Publishing, Harrow Weald, HA3 5JL
Printed by CS Graphics, Singapore

Title Page: Emerging from Vouvray Tunnel, this Atlantique train is about to cross the viaduct over the River Loire. *SNCF-CAV*
Title Page inset: Eurostar power car at the head of its train in Bourg-St-Maurice station against the background of the French Alps. *Brian Perren*

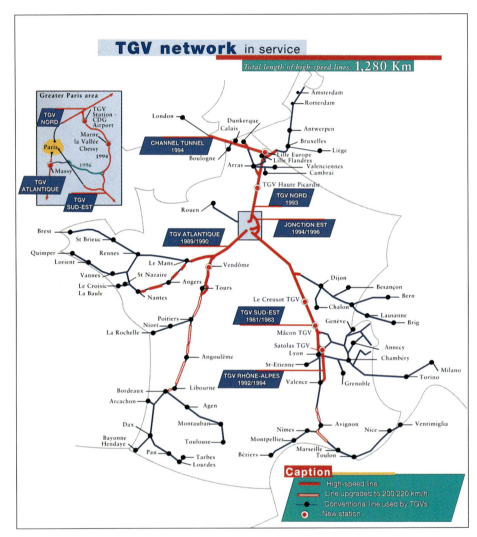

TGV network in service

Total length of high-speed lines: 1,280 Km

Greater Paris area

TGV NORD · TGV Station - CDG Airport · Marne la Vallée Chessy 1994 · Paris · 1996 · Massy · TGV ATLANTIQUE · TGV SUD-EST

Amsterdam
Rotterdam
London
Dunkerque
Calais
Antwerpen
Bruxelles
Liège
CHANNEL TUNNEL 1994
Boulogne
Lille Europe
Lille Flandres
Arras
Valenciennes
Cambrai
TGV Haute Picardie
TGV NORD 1993
Rouen
JONCTION EST 1994/1996
Brest
St Brieuc
TGV ATLANTIQUE 1989/1990
Quimper
Lorient
Rennes
Le Mans
Vendôme
Dijon
Besançon
Vannes
St Nazaire
Angers
Tours
Bern
Le Croisic
La Baule
Nantes
Le Creusot TGV
Chalon
Lausanne
Poitiers
TGV SUD-EST 1981/1983
Genève
Brig
Niort
La Rochelle
Mâcon TGV
Satolas TGV
Lyon
Annecy
Chambéry
Angoulême
St-Etienne
Milano
TGV RHÔNE-ALPES 1992/1994
Valence
Torino
Bordeaux
Libourne
Grenoble
Arcachon
Agen
Montauban
Dax
Nîmes
Avignon
Nice
Ventimiglia
Bayonne
Hendaye
Toulouse
Montpellier
Pau
Tarbes
Lourdes
Béziers
Marseille
Toulon

Caption
High-speed line
Line upgraded to 200/220 km/h
Conventional line used by TGVs
New station

SNCF:

INTRODUCTION

Welcome to TGV Handbook second edition. The pace of TGV development – in France as well as its near neighbours, Asia and the United States – since the first edition was published in Autumn 1993 has been such that this second edition is essentially a new publication.

Many of the projects described in the first edition have now come to fruition – in particular the Nord Europe high-speed line from Paris to the Channel Tunnel and the Belgian frontier. Eurostar can now take you from Paris to London in three hours and by the end of 1997 THALYS will take you from Paris to the centre of Brussels in less than 90 minutes. Regional Eurostars will soon operate to points beyond London and THALYS operates to Cologne as well as Amsterdam. New infrastructure to reduce journey times and increase rail capacity is to be built in Britain, Belgium, Germany, and the Netherlands.

With the completion of the Jonction and Rhône Alpes lines, which bypass Paris and Lyon, French Railways now has a continuous 270–300 km/h high-speed railway from Calais to Valence – a total of 1070 kilometres (660 miles). By 2000 – when TGV Méditerranée is open from St-Marcel-les-Valence to Marseille – the length of this axis from the English Channel to the Mediterranean – will be 1,294 kilometres (804 miles).

While the Paris Sud Est and Atlantique lines were affordable in both corporate and social-benefit terms, the cost of such new lines has now risen to the extent that SNCF has had to curtail much of its ambitious 1993 High Speed Master Plan. A few key projects – including the preliminary stage of TGV Est from Paris to the Moselle Valley – have survived. Responsibility for the development of high-speed and other infrastructure projects has now passed from SNCF to a new state-owned organisation Réseau Ferré de France. Established in February 1997, RFF is to be a small policy-making organisation; responsibility for day-to-day operation and maintenance of the national network and other engineering aspects has been contracted back to SNCF.

On-going research and development has improved trainset performance and passenger comfort. Although the basic format of two power cars enclosing a rake of articulated trailers has been retained, technical progress has been significant. Whereas the original Paris Sud Est sets had 12 traction motors with 6,450 kW installed power for a 360-seat 270 km/h train, a Réseau set has 8,800 kW installed power for a 300 km/h train with slightly more seats. With aluminium-bodied double-deck trailer cars the latest Duplex train, with 8,800 kW installed power, carries 516 passengers at 300 km/h, an economic improvement of around 40%. The Duplex power-car bodyshell has also been used for the four-voltage THALYS trains to work in to Germany as well as Belgium and The Netherlands; and it will also be the test-bed for the TGV New Generation trains able to run up to 350 km/h or even higher. Tilting TGVs are now a possibility.

While the responsibility for the accuracy of the text remains with the author, I would like to thank all of those many people in the railway industry – particularly at SNCF – who have gladly provided information, help and encouragement for the production of this book. Without this assistance TGV Handbook Second Edition would not have been possible.

Brian Perren

One of the journey highlights of the Paris Sud Est line is the climb from Cluny going south and from Mâcon going north to Col Du Bois Clair summit. To avoid tunnelling through the Burgundy hills, the line is engineered with gradients of 3.5% in both directions. The picture shows a southbound PSE train approaching the summit on newly ballasted track. *Brian Perren*

PARIS-SUD EST

We begin our survey of TGV – Trains à Grande Vitesse – with a brief history of the different routes. The decision to build the Paris Sud Est (PSE) line from Paris to Lyon evolved from two basic factors – the recognition by SNCF that rail could only remain competitive with the growing autoroute network and improved airline services if centre-to-centre journey times were drastically reduced, and even with modest rates of growth, capacity on key strategic routes would be unable to cope with future levels of business.

While significant sections of the Paris – Bordeaux line had a potential speed of 200 km/h and even higher, this was not the case on the classic Paris-Lyon-Méditerranée (PLM) route. Serving 40% of the entire population of France, the PLM is a route of major strategic importance. As well as serving Dijon, Lyon, Avignon, Montpellier, Marseille and Nice, it provides access to the French Alps, Switzerland (Lausanne via Vallorbe and Geneva via Mâcon), Italy via Modane and Spain via Port-Bou. By the start of the 1970s a situation had developed where continuing growth of around 4% per year had led to the realisation that the route would soon be saturated to the extent that further growth and future levels of business would be constrained by route capacity.

There were two factors – track capacity and line speeds. For the greater part of its 315 km (196 mile) route from Paris to Dijon the PLM has four tracks, but there were two critical two-track sections between St-Florentin and Les Laumes (83 km/52 miles) and Blaisy Bas to Dijon (26 km/16 miles) where pathing 160 km/h (100 mph) passenger trains and slower moving freights was an on-going problem. While there were long sections of route fit for 160 km/h, the general topography and track geometry was such as to rule out major infrastructure upgrading except at prohibitive cost. Also, the cost of doubling the 4 km (2fi-mile) Blaisy Bas Tunnel and the two-track section down into Dijon was not a practical possibility. Even though the route had been electrified for a little over 10 years, its practical operating capacity would soon be reached.

Given the impossibility of upgrading the PLM, SNCF prepared plans for a new high-speed railway which would link Paris, Dijon, Lyon and South East France. The cost of the new line was equal to about 40% of the cost of upgrading the PLM where this was theoretically possible. With almost all long-distance passenger traffic transferred to the new line, ample capacity would then be available for freight and other lower-speed traffic remaining on the PLM.

However, unlike the Japanese Shinkansen – which is a purpose-built self-contained system – the PSE line was designed as an increment to and part of the existing national network. Thus, after using the high speed line the new TGV trains would be able to run through to all other parts of the SNCF electrified system. Not only would this obviate the enormous environmental disturbance and cost of building new tracks into the centre of Paris, Lyon and other cities, but all of South East France would benefit from reduced journey times. This concept has been applied to subsequent TGV projects.

Construction of the PSE line started at the end of 1976 and was completed in two stages – the southern section from Sathonay/Aisy to St-Florentin in September 1981 and the northern section from St-Florentin to Lieusaint in September 1983.

Construction of nuclear power stations and railway electrification were two essential features of the strategy adopted by the French Government in the wake of the 1973 international oil crisis. This Paris–Montpellier service, formed by PSE Unit 13, is passing the Cruas nuclear power station at L'Homme d'Armes near Montélimar. *Michael Collins*

To reach Lieusaint – 29 km (18.3 miles) from the Gare-de-Lyon terminus in Paris – TGVs use the classic PLM tracks through Villeneuve-St-Georges and Brunoy shared with other passenger and freight traffic. At Lieusaint southbound TGVs diverge to the left and northbound trains pass over the other classic tracks through a complicated two-stage grade separation to join the main track into the Gare-de-Lyon without conflicting with other traffic.

With the opening of the Jonction Oeust (West) in June 1996 – the western branch of the Paris interconnection line described later – the start of the PSE has been moved to a new location at Créteil, only 9.4 km (5.8 miles) from the Gare-de-Lyon. In other words, the Jonction Oeust is also an extension of the original PSE line. At Créteil the pair of main tracks to/from the Gare-de-Lyon have been re-aligned towards the new railway.

Almost immediately along the Jonction Ouest route the tracks pass over the Grande Ceinture line (the radial rail route around Paris mostly used by freight trains) at Valenton. Here there is another connection – Bifurcation Massy – enabling TGVs from the Atlantique line at Massy to access the new route. Because this railway passes through residential areas, part of the infrastructure – Limeil-Brevannes (1,635 m) and Villecresines (2,199 m) – has been built in cut-and-cover tunnels to minimise environmental disturbance.

At Coubert – 21 km (13 miles) from Créteil – trains bound for the Sud Est take the west-to-south side of the triangular junction layout, from where they head south to join the original PSE alignment at Crisenoy (sometimes referred to as Moisenay). By the old route out of Paris, Crisenoy is 17 km from Lieusaint and 46.4 km (28.8 miles) from the Gare-de-Lyon; the distance from the Gare-de-Lyon by the new line from Créteil is 49.1 km (30.5 miles), 2.7 km longer.

From the start of the original line at Lieusaint the route is through open country, across the plain of Brie, then close to but avoiding the towns of Montereau and Sens. For the 70 or so km from Lieusaint to a point near Sens, the new A5 autoroute has been built alongside the railway. At St-Florentin – 117 km (72.7 miles) from Lieusaint – there is a 160 km/h junction enabling trains to/from Paris to join the high-speed line in the Lyon direction. From 1981 to 1983, before the complete route was opened, this junction was the temporary end of the PSE line; it is now mostly used in emergencies but also by a sporadic TGV between Melun and Marseille.

At Pasilly, 45 km (30 miles) beyond St-Florentin, the branch to Aisy parts company with the main line on turnouts designed for 220 km/h (137 mph). This short 15 km (9.3 mile) spur is the route to Dijon and thence through Dôle to Besançon, Vallorbe and Switzerland. The first of the only two intermediate stations is at Le Creusot-Montchanin (274 km/170 miles) from Lieusaint and the second is at Mâcon-Loché (334 km/207 miles).

Just beyond Mâcon TGV station, before the viaduct over the River Saône, there are two bi-directional single-track connections with the PLM line. The first is from the high-speed line Lyon direction to the PLM northbound to Mâcon Ville station to Dijon and Paris by the classic route. The other is from Lyon (PLM) to the high-speed line to Mâcon-Loché TGV station and thence northbound to Paris; Mâcon TGV postal station is located on this short spur. Apart from the Cavaillon-Paris postal TGV which calls at the postal station, these two connections are only used for emergencies.

Immediately beyond the River Sâone viaduct is the high-speed junction – Bifurcation Savoie – for the 8 kilometre spur to Pont-de-Veyle for the classic line to Bourg-en-Bresse, Geneva and the French Alpes.

At Montany – 42.8 km (26.5 miles) from Bifurcation Savoie – there is another major change to the original route. Here the tracks have been realigned to form the interface with TGV Rhône Alpes, the next stage of SNCF's plans to extend the PSE line to the South of France, described in Chapters 5 and 31. In the new layout the main tracks form the new route; the old southbound track to Lyon has been repositioned passing over the new layout by grade separation. The end of the PSE line as originally built is at Sathony – 393.8 km (244.7 miles) from the end of the original route at Lieusaint – and only 5.5 km south of Montany where the new Rhône Alpes line starts.

Following the opening of the Rhône Alpes line, Paris–Chambéry trains, including the twice-daily Paris–Milan service, are routed via Satolas, St-Quentin-Fallavier and the single-line branch from St-André-le-Gaz to Chambéry. Here the morning service from Chambéry to Paris is passing through the station loop at St-Béron-la-Bridoire. *Brian Perren*

TGV Duplex trains are now in fleet service between Paris and Lyon. This Paris to Lyon service is passing through the long junction layout at St-Florentin; for a short distance at this point the northbound and south-bound tracks are on a separate alignment. *Brian Perren.*

Because the most suitable route for the new railway into the Lyon area was through Sathonay and also because the increase in traffic necessitated a major reorganisation of train working through the greater Lyon area, a major new station was built at Part-Dieu to cope with the volume of TGV traffic.

Thanks to the ability of modern electric traction to cope with steeper gradients and of low-slung rolling stock to sustain high standards of ride comfort, the PSE high-speed line was engineered to standards well beyond the parameters hitherto applicable to classic railway routes. With railway engineers now able to work within similar parameters to motorway builders, the choice of an unobtrusive route through the French countryside – where the population density is much less than Britain, Germany or the Netherlands – was not too difficult. Sound protection barriers have been installed to minimise the disturbance to villages close to the line of route. In 1969 a study group was formed to consider the possibilities of combining railway and road infrastructure where this was possible. This policy has been implemented. As mentioned, for 70 or so kilometres from Lieusaint to a point near to the town of Sens the PSE runs alongside the new A5 autoroute; also, but for a shorter distance, the new 15 km section of the N79 cross-country road has been built alongside the railway over Col du Bois Clair summit north of Mâcon.

Although the PSE is designed for a maximum speed of 300 km/h (186.4 mph), the present maximum speed is 270 km/h (167.8 mph). To achieve these speeds the minimum radius curve is 4,000 metres, the spacing between the overhead catenary supports is 13 meters, the track centres are 3.60 metres from the catenary supports and the space between the track centres is 4.2 metres. UIC 60 kg rails are laid on deep ballast. To minimise track wear, all TGV trainsets have been designed with a 17-tonne maximum axle-load. After 14 years in service, a project to replace the ballast and points and crossings between Mâcon and St-Florentin was started in 1995.

To obviate tunnelling the engineers opted for a ruling gradient of 3.5% (1 in 28.5). This applies for about 3 km near KP (kilometre point) 273 north of Le Creusot-Montchanin station and at the aforementioned Col du Bois Clair north of Mâcon. Here the climb to the summit is about four kilometres southbound and six kilometres northbound.

A new station was built at Lyon Part-Dieu for the Paris Sud Est line. Located in the centre of the French national network, the station is a major interchange between TGVs, long-distance and Regional services. *French Railways*

Inaugural 'Line De Coeur' Zürich to Paris TGV via Bern and Dijon awaits its 0713 departure at Zürich Hbf.
Brian Perren

Lac du Bourget near Aix-les-Bains in the French Alps is a favoured spot for rail photographers. Coming from Paris this repainted PSE unit is bound for Aix-les-Bains where it will reverse to reach its destination at Annecy.
Brian Perren

Because of the much higher speeds on the new railway, SNCF decided to install TVM 300 computer-based in-cab signalling instead of conventional lateral or lineside signalling used on classic routes. (see Chapter 14). Visible signs of this system are the blue and yellow markerboards which indicate the start of each block section for the driver. Signalling headway is at present five minutes between successive trains; plans are being developed to reduce this headway to four minutes in association with an increase in line speed from 270 to 300 km/h. The 417 km (259.1 miles) of route is signalled for full reversible working on both tracks at the full line speed in each direction. A 220 km/h restriction applies for trains diverging from or joining the main line at Pasilly and Bifurcation Savoie (Mâcon). Kilometre points – 0.0 km starting at Lieusaint – mark out the route.

Bi-directional working can be implemented through 220 km/h (136.7 mph) crossovers located at average distances of around 22 km (13.8 miles) throughout the route. These crossovers are activated by satellite units – *poste à relais a transit souple* (PRS) – controlled from the central operations centre at Paris. The PSE has 28 such PRS units which are numbered from 10 to 27 on the main line; the other is on the Pasilly branch. They are also used as reference points for the compilation of train schedules and calculation of point-to-point running times for the guidance of drivers.

When TGVs pass between the classic and TGV tracks, drivers have to change from 1.5kV dc to 25kV ac power supplies and engage (or disengage) the TVM cab-signalling system. This Atlantique unit at Lieusaint is passing the marker-boards instructing the driver to be ready to change over to TVM cab-signalling and engage radio channel 9.
Brian Perren

At busy times – such as the winter ski peak – one of the yellow-liveried postal power cars may be used to deputise in a passenger set. This Sunday ski service is just leaving Albertville bound for Paris with ski passengers. *Brian Perren*

Because of the length of the PSE line and as there are only two intermediate passenger stations, special facilities are necessary to cope with a train failure or other operating incidents. If it is necessary to take a failed train out of service it can be pushed by a following train either to Le Creusot-Montchanin or Mâcon-Loché stations or to one of three emergency stations at Marolles (PRS12), Vaumort (PRS14), and La Cour-D'Arcenay (PRS19). Each has a refuge siding able to cope with four standard PSE trainsets where there is a walkway enabling passengers to de-train and transfer to another train in complete safety.

Traction power supply on the PSE (and all other TGV lines) is 25 kV ac. However, as a large part of the SNCF network was electrified on the old 1.5 kV monophase direct current (dc) system before the more efficient 25 kV ac system was developed for rail use from the late 1950s, provision has to be made for TGV trainsets (and other traction units) to run on both systems in order to access all parts of the national network. (The cost of converting existing dc lines to ac power supplies is prohibitive). As all entry points on to the PSE are electrified on the old 1.5 kV dc system, trains have to pass through a short neutral section before they can change to the 25 kV ac system. This change is made at full line speed. The driver lowers the dc pantograph, coasts through a short neutral section, and then raises the ac pantograph when the train is under the new system. The changeover points are denoted by a series of lineside markerboards. Power supplies for the PSE line are taken from the French National Grid and distributed through six sub-stations.

Two-unit Paris to Lyon service negotiates point work to arrive at Lyon Part-Dieu. *Brian Perren*

This Duplex northbound service is about to start the long 3.5% climb north of Mâcon to Col-du-Bois summit. *Brian Perren*

Paris Gare-de-Lyon terminal station; note the *Accueil* customer information point. *Brian Perren*

Despite the length of the journey, TGVs do good business along the Côte D'Azure coastal resorts. This Paris-bound PSE set is passing through Theoule Sur Mer. *Brian Perren*

Paris-bound PSE service heads through Bollène north of Orange in Provence. The 21 kilometres between Bollène and Pierrelatte is one of the sections of the Rhône Valley main line where TGVs are authorised to run at 200 km/h. *Michael Collins*

Although the 10 three-voltage Réseau PBA trainsets are primarily intended for use between Paris, Brussels and Amsterdam, they are sometimes used for services from Brussels Midi to the South of France. This north-bound service is shown approaching the junction layout at St-Florentin. *Brian Perren*

Réseau double-unit Sunday ski service from Paris Gare-de-Lyon to Bourg-St-Maurice sets down passengers at Landry. *Brian Perren*

Left: Access to Annecy – the popular all-season Haute Savoie lake resort – is by the single-line route from Aix-les-Bains. Bound for Annecy, this PSE unit has just joined the branch at the north end of Aix-les-Bains station where it is in the process of changing from 1.5kV dc to 25kV ac power supplies. In the 1950s the Annecy branch was the test bed for evaluating the then new 25kV ac power supply system. *Brian Perren*

THE ATLANTIQUE LINE

Encouraged by the technical and commercial success of the PSE line, SNCF started work on its next high-speed project – the Atlantique line from Paris to the West and South West of France – in February 1985. Had agreement to build the Channel Tunnel been reached earlier, TGV Nord Europe – the next in order of priority – would have been the second new route to have been built. By 1982 the SNCF board had approved the Atlantique project and submitted the proposals for Government approval; this was received on 1 July 1982 and the 'Public Utility' process was initiated. As a 'Declaration of Public Utility' gives wide powers to a state-owned concern – such as the compulsory purchase of land – the consultation process is very thorough but shorter than is the case in other countries. TGV Atlantique was declared a 'Public Utility' on 25 May 1984.

Like that for the PSE, the case for the Atlantique line was based on the inability of the existing infrastructure, out of Paris (Montparnasse) towards Le Mans and from Paris (Austerlitz) towards Orléans and Tours, to cope with future levels of growth. Not only would the cost of upgrading these two routes be very high, but 200 km/h would have been the maximum speed which could have been achieved.

Accordingly, SNCF looked for an alternative solution in the form of a new line which could carry the combined traffic from Montparnasse to the West and from Austerlitz to the South West on a common section of route to a point where the new line would plug into the existing railway network. Detailed studies showed that, by using the infrastructure of an abandoned inter-city project from Montparnasse to Chartres known as the Gallardon line, there was potential access straight into Montparnasse station in the centre of Paris. Thus, whereas the PSE line originally started 29.4 kilometres (18.3 miles) from the centre of Paris, Atlantique infrastructure starts at Bagneux, just 6.4 km (4 miles) from Montparnasse station. Comprising 280 km (174 miles) of route, the Y-shaped line divides into two separate branches at Courtalain – the Western (Brittany) branch to Connerré where it joins the classic Paris Montparnasse-Le Mans line and the South West (Aquitaine) branch which joins the classic Paris Austerlitz-Bordeaux line at Monts just west of Tours.

While the basic principles of the Atlantique project are the same as the PSE, there are a number of significant differences between the two routes. The topography of this part of France is such that the line is engineered with 4,200-metre minimum-radius curves and the ruling gradient is 2.5% (1 in 40) compared with the PSE's 3.5% (1 in 28fi). On the Atlantique route the TVM300 cab-signalling system was designed for a 300 km/h (186.4 mph) line speed with a four-minute operating headway. There was a new type of catenary design and the superstructure dimensions were also changed, but the space between track centres was retained at 4.2 metres. Whereas there are no tunnels on the PSE, there are major tunnel and cut-and-cover sections on the Atlantique line.

Once clear of Montparnasse station layout, from Bagneux TGVs have their own pair of dedicated tracks on the left (outbound) side of the multi-track railway. While the old Gallardon line gave SNCF a good route into the centre of Paris, it was by now surrounded by heavily-populated housing developments which were not there when the line was conceived in the 1930s. To provide appropriate levels of environmental protection – particularly against noise – the first 30 or so kilometres from Paris is mostly in tunnel or cut-and-cover sections. Public acceptance of the Atlantique project would not have been possible without this so-called 'green corridor'.

TGV Atlantique

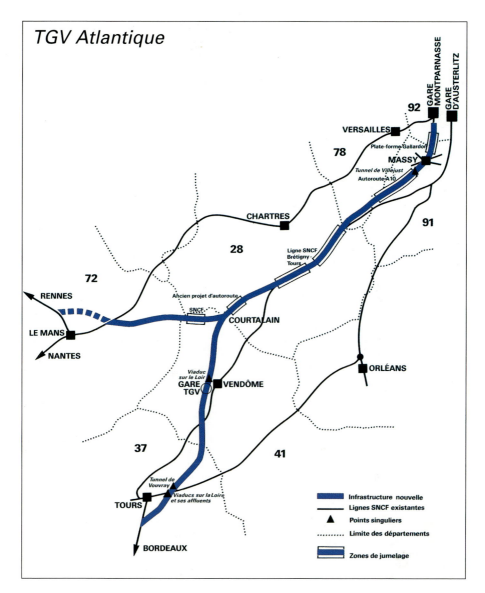

There are two double-track tunnels – Fontenay (475 metres) and Sceaux (827 metres) – plus covered sections between the start of the new line at Bagneux and the TGV railhead station at Massy. At Massy – which is one of three such TGV railhead stations in the Ile-de-France Region – there is a junction with the Paris Grande Ceinture radial railroute so that TGVs to or from the West/South West bound for the North or the South East can reach the new Jonction Oeust (West) at Valenton. (The Valenton Junction is – somewhat misleadingly – referred to as Bifurcation Massy). Partly in cut-and-cover, Massy TGV station has two long platform loops able to accommodate a 475.18 metre two-unit Atlantique train; two retaining walls protect the platforms from the noise and wind from trains passing through the centre tracks at 200 km/h.

Departure hall at the modernised
Paris Montparnasse station; note
the self-service automatic ticket
and reservation machines.
Brian Perren

Because the Gallardon route out
of Paris Montparnasse passes
through sensitive residential
areas, sections of the line have
been covered over to provide a
'Green Corridor'. *SNCF-CAV*

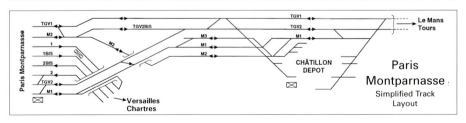

Westbound Atlantique service gathers speed at Km 14 as it approaches the east end of Massy TGV station. The tracks on the extreme left and right of the picture are the connections with the Grande Ceinture Line, the route for Atlantique TGVs bound for the Sud Est or Nord Europe routes to reach the Jonction Oeust at Valenton. The markerboard on the left is 'Baissey Panto Distance' – advising drivers that a voltage change from 25 kV ac to 1.5 kV dc is about to be necessary for the Grande Ceinture tracks. *Brian Perren*

There is a short break between the end of the Massy covered section and the next similar section at Villebon before the line enters the single-bore 4,800 metre (3 miles) tunnel, the dimensions of which allow passage at 270 km/h (167.8 mph). There is a final 1,273-metre covered section – line speed 300 km/h – at Briis-sous-Forges before the line reaches the end of the Paris outer residential area at KP 29. For the next 15 kilometres the line runs alongside the A10 Autoroute Aquitaine, diverging near the village of Ponthévrard, from where the railway alignment is through open country; for 50 or so kilometres the line continues alongside the old single-track classic line from Paris to Vendôme.

As mentioned, the Brittany (West) and Aquitaine (South West) branches part company at Courtalain, 130 kilometres (80.7 miles) from Paris, where the westbound Brittany track passes over the eastbound Aquitaine track on a long flyover. Designed for 270 km/h line speed in each direction, the junction layout extends for about 4,000 metres (2.5 miles).

The distance through open country from Courtalain to Connerré – the present end of the Brittany branch – is 51 kilometres (31.7 miles). For the present, the tracks at Connerré are aligned to join the classic line for the final 12 kilometres (7.5 miles) to Le Mans; this section has been upgraded to 220 km/h. Space has been left to link-up with the Brittany Branch extension to Sablé – TGV Bretagne-Pays de le Loire – described in Chapter 24.

From Courtalain Junction the Aquitaine branch runs through open country until a point north of the town of Vendôme. To serve the town – hitherto only served by a sparse and very slow diesel train service on a secondary route between Paris and Tours – the local authority part-funded a new Vendôme TGV railhead station. There are two platform loops; the through 300 km/h tracks pass through the centre of the station. Towards the end of the line – as the route approaches the Tours area – there was an interesting environmental issue. SNCF's proposal for a tunnel under the famed Vouvray vineyards did not find favour with the local wine-growing community who feared vibrations would affect the quality of the grapes. But following a series of tests the local community was reassured and accepted the tunnel proposal. After passage of Vouvray Tunnel (1,510 metres), the railway is close to the Tours area; 1,500 metres beyond the south-end of the tunnel is the first of a series of connecting junctions between the high-speed line and the classic railway network.

As reference to the diagram opposite shows, the Tours network is complex. The first station to serve the town was a dead-end, and it subsequently became necessary to build an avoiding line, and a second station at St Pierre-de-Corps, so that through Paris-Bordeaux services could serve the town without the need to reverse and change locomotives in the town station. Shuttle trains are provided between St Pierre-des-Corps and Tours town station. To give good journey times between Paris, Bordeaux and the South West, it was decided to take the new railway on an alignment well to the east of the town where it joins the classic Paris-Bordeaux line at Monts. This alignment has regard to the long-term plan to extend the Atlantique line to Bordeaux – TGV Aquitaine. Because of the number of train movements in the St Pierre-des-Corps area – the station is located next to a busy freight yard – there is a need for more capacity in the area. Accordingly, the last 17 kilometres of the Atlantique line is designed to carry both high-speed and classic passenger and freight trains; consequently it is equipped with modified lineside signalling and power supplies are 1.5 kV dc.

There is a series of junctions in the Tours area. TGVs from Paris calling at St Pierre-des-Corps or terminating at Tours leave the high-speed line by the 160 km/h St Pierre-des-Corps chord; trains from the old line from Paris via Orléans can join the high-speed line by the Montlouis chord and trains from the South West can reach St Pierre-des-Corps by the third chord La Ville Aux Dames. TGVs between Paris and Bordeaux calling at St Pierre-des-Corps join the classic route to the South at Monts.

From the Tours end of Vouvray Tunnel to the junction for St Pierre-des-Corps – a distance of 2.5 kilometres – the line passes over a series of viaducts and embankments. The first of these – Vouvray Viaduct – starts at the tunnel mouth; the second viaduct crosses La Cisse River; and the third takes the railway across the River Loire – one of the great rivers of France. There is a further series of viaducts and embankments beyond the St Pierre-des-Corps group of junctions – the most important of which is across Le Cher River.

To emphasise its role in the Atlantique network, the Tour – St-Pierre-des-Corps shuttle train is painted in TGV Atlantique livery. *Brian Perren*

The construction of these bridges is in pre-stressed concrete with spans up to 63 metres. The exit from Le Cher Viaduct leads to a short cut-and-cover section. At Monts Junction – 230 kilometres (142.9 miles) from Paris Montparnasse – the Atlantique line joins the classic Paris-Bordeaux line.

The Atlantique line is equipped for two-way working at full line speed in each direction with 220 km/h crossovers positioned at frequent intervals. There are three emergency refuge sidings for dealing with failed trains or other problems; two of these – Saint Ledger PRS 14 and Dangau PRS 16 – are located between Paris and Courtalain and the third, Dollon PRS 32, is on the Brittany branch. Vendôme station provides the necessary emergency cover on the Aquitaine branch.

Once clear of the Paris Montparnasse station layout and on to dedicated TGV tracks, the line speed increases to 200 km/h to a point beyond Massy station, to 270 km/h for the Villebon-Villejust section from where – with the exception of Courtalain Junction restricted to 270 km/h – 300 km/h applies to Vouvray Tunnel, restricted to 270 km/h; 270 km/h then applies to the end of the Acquitaine branch at Monts. Line speed on the Brittany branch from Courtalain to Connerré is 300 km/h. As the classic network from Paris to Le Mans and Bordeaux was originally electrified at 1.5 kV dc there are a number of voltage changeover points. TGVs change to 25 kV ac in Sceaux Tunnel 7.5 kilometres from Paris; changeovers from 25 kV ac back to 1.5 kV dc are at St Pierre-des-Corps Junction near Tours and the end of the Brittany branch at Connerré.

Atlantique line distances are measured not from the start of the new line proper at Bagneux, but from Paris Montparnasse terminal station. Also, the Brittany and Aquitaine branches are measured continuously from Montparnasse and not separately.

Formed by a single Atlantique unit the 1426 Le Croisic to Paris Montparnasse passes La Baule-Escoublac. *Ken Harris*

This Rennes to Paris Montparnasse train calls en route at Le Mans, one of many stations to have been refurbished for the launch of the TGV services. *Brian Perren*

Westbound Paris – Bordeaux Atlantique service approaches Vouvray Tunnel. *Brian Perren*

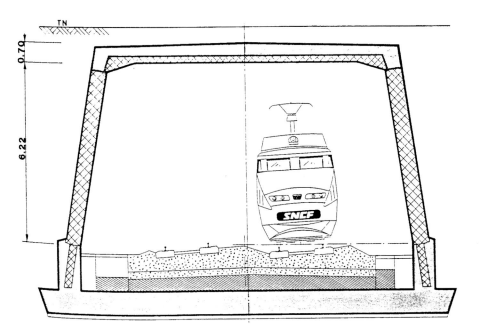

SNCF's first Paris to Lyon high-speed line was built without any tunnels, but it was necessary to build several different types of tunnel to meet the particular characteristics of the Atlantique line. A pre-fabrication principle was used for the double-track Fontenay-Massy 'Green Corridor' section where the line speed is 200 km/h. Single-bore tunnels, line speed 270 km/h, were built at Villejust and deep cut-and-cover was used for the double-track tunnel at Briis-sous-Forges (line speed 300 km/h). *SNCF*

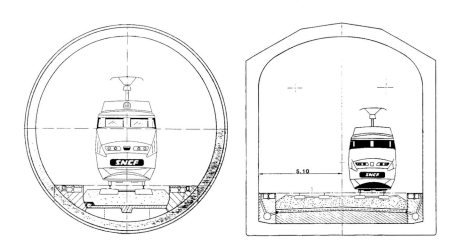

TGV NORD EUROPE

While it would convey a significant volume of French domestic traffic originating in the Nord-Pas de Calais region, TGV Nord Europe – together with the Belgian high-speed line, the Paris TGV bypass line and the Channel Tunnel, all of which are described later – is the essential link in the emerging European high-speed rail network. The business case for the line is based on traffic flows from three sources – domestic travel between Northern France, Paris and the other French regions; international traffic from the UK through the Channel Tunnel; and international traffic on the Paris – Brussels – Köln (Cologne) – Amsterdam (PBKA) axis. 'Declaration of Public Utility' was given on 23 April 1985.

Totalling 333 km (207 miles) of route, TGV Nord Europe is equipped with TVM 430 cab-signalling allowing a maximum speed of 300 km/h (186.4 mph) with a three-minute headway between trains. Maximum potential speed is, however, 320 km/h (198.8 mph), but at present there are no plans to operate at this speed. Ruling gradient is 2.5% (1 in 40) and the minimum-radius curve is 3,520 metres. To allow the higher 320 km/h maximum speed, the width of the infrastructure base is 13.9 metres and the space between track centres is 4.5 metres. There are no tunnels, but for the passage of the Lille area the line has been built in cut-and-cover for environmental protection purposes.

The Nord Europe high-speed line starts at Gonesse – 16 kilometres (10 miles) out of Paris Nord terminal station – where the new line connects with the classic Creil main line through 220 km/h (136.7 mph) grade-separated junctions. At Vémars – 11 kilometres from Gonesse – there is the triangular grade-separated junction with the Paris Interconnexion TGV by-pass line, now referred to as La Jonction. The main junction, which is designed for 220 km/h, is north-south; the triangle is completed by a two grade-separated chords enabling trains from the south to reach Le Landy depot or the Gare du Nord terminal station. This connection is mainly for emergencies, but it is sometimes used during the ski season for trains from Paris to the Alpes to relieve pressure on peak days at the Gare-de-Lyon.

Beyond Vémars the alignment is through open country to a point near Chevrières, from where it shares the same infrastructure alongside the Autoroute du Nord for the ensuing 85 or so kilometres (53 miles) to the outskirts of Arras. During the planning consultation procedures there was considerable pressure from Amiens to route the Nord Europe line through the town rather than SNCF's preferred choice through Lille. The case for the Amiens routeing was poor. Not only is the Lille conurbation one of the four largest in France, but is close to the Belgian border. To placate Amiens, SNCF built a TGV railhead station in Picardie close to the junction of the nearby N29 trunk road and the A1 autoroute. The N29 also gives access to Péronne and St-Quentin. Unkindly referred to as a 'station in a beetroot field', TGV Haute-Picardie – 110 kilometres (68.4 miles) from Gonesse – is nonetheless a stylish station; there are two long platforms and ample space for parking. SNCF runs a connecting bus service to Amiens.

Bifurcation de Croisilles – 148 kilometres (92 miles) from Gonesse – is the access junction for the 10.8-kilometre (6.7-mile) branch to the classic line allowing TGVs to reach Arras. This is the route from Paris Nord to Arras, Dunkerque (via Hazebrouck) and Valenciennes and for some cross-country services to/from Lille Europe which make calls at Arras and Douai. There is a second single-track junction to/from Arras towards Lille a few kilometres north of the town station on the classic route to Lille which joins the high-speed line at Km 162; this is primarily for emergency purposes.

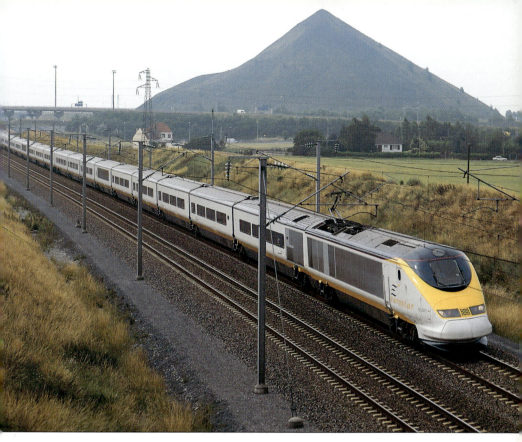

Paris Nord to Waterloo International Eurostar at 300 km/h on the TGV Nord Europe line near Dourges.
Colin Marsden

An acceptable passage through Lille was the subject of much discussion. SNCF's first idea was for a TGV railhead station on the outskirts of the city, but this did not find favour. Recognising the business and social benefits which the Lille conurbation would gain from the European high-speed network, community businessmen led by the dynamic mayor of Lille – former Prime Minister Pierre Mauroy – persuaded SNCF to route the Nord Europe TGV line through the centre of the city as part of the massive Euralille project.

Located on reclaimed land in the space between the existing SNCF terminal station (renamed Lille Flandres) and the new Lille Europe sub-surface TGV station, Euralille covers an area of 173 acres with potential to expand to 288 acres. An example of private and public section collaboration favoured by the French, Euralille cost 5.3 billion francs – 1.6 billion from private and 3.7 billion from public funds. There are 45,000 sq metres of offices; 31,000 sq metres of shops; 200 homes have been built and 700 are planned. Two hotels provide support for the Grand Palais exhibition centre (20,000 sq metres of space) and there are two concert halls.

Even without Euralille the size and potential of Lille with a population of around 1.0 million people was too significant to be ignored, whereas the population of Arras was only 132,000. Also, Lille was close to the location on the border favoured by the Belgians for the continuation through to Brussels. Moreover, the route from Paris to Lille was an easy choice – for it would run alongside the existing A1 Autoroute du Nord for a significant distance.

Passage of the Lille area starts at the Fretin triangle (Raccordement de Fretin) 198 kilometres (123 miles) from Gonesse – where the Calais and Belgian branches of the route part company. The Fretin triangle consists of the following routeings – from Paris to the interface with TGV Belge at Wannehain, the France-Belgium frontier; Paris to Lille, Calais, the Channel Tunnel and Britain; and the route to/from TGV Belge into Lille, Calais, the Channel Tunnel and Britain. Line speeds are 300 km/h for the main Paris – Brussels route and 220 km/h for the four connecting chords. As TGVs have to start to reduce speed for the passage of Lille Europe station, the Fretin layout was designed to give the higher speed towards Belgium and the lower speeds towards Lille. The Belgian frontier is just nine kilometres (5.6 miles) from the north side of the Fretin triangle where TGV Nord Europe crosses the frontier, continuing as the Belgian high-speed line. Nord Europe distances are measured from Gonesse KP 0.0 to the Belgium frontier KP 209.8; the Calais branch is measured separately starting at Fretin Sud KP 198 which is KP 0.0 on the Calais branch.

Well beyond the centre of Lille at KP 26 the line is once again in open country and the line speed is back to 300 km/h. At Hondeghem, 56 kilometres (34.8 miles) from Fretin, there is a crossover leading to the single-track Cassel chord for access to the Arras-Dunkerque classic line. With the construction of the Channel Tunnel and TGV Nord Europe the railways in the Calais area have been transformed. To serve the area there is a railhead station – Calais-Fréthun TGV – 326 kilometres from Paris Nord. There are two platforms for Eurostar international trains and a separate section for local trains on the classic

There is a single-track connection at Roeux (KM 161.9) from the Paris – Arras classic line and TGV Nord Europe

Arras-Boulogne-Calais line and for TGVs between Paris Nord and Calais or Boulogne. Boulogne TGVs have to reverse here. The Nord Europe TGV line finishes at 113.8 kilometres (70.7 miles) from Fretin from where the tracks continue for 2 kilometres (1.24 miles) to the French Channel Tunnel Portal.

The route is signalled for full bi-directional working on both tracks at the full 300 km/h line speed, but speeds through the cut-and-cover section on either side of Lille Europe station are restricted to 200 km/h (125 mph) for aerodynamic reasons. Designed for 220 km/h (136.7 mph) transits, 287-metre single-lead crossovers are located at strategic points along the line, the spacing of which varies from 10 to 25 kilometres; average spacing is around 12 kilometres. Because of the length of the trains and the minimum radius curves necessary for very high speeds (200 km/h and above) junction and station layouts are much longer than those on classic railways. Typically these single-lead junctions are around 650 to 700 metres long. The end-to-end distance between the bidirectional approach crossovers at Haute Picardie station is no less than 2.6 kilometres (1.6 miles); similarly the track layout at Lille Europe is 3.7 kilometres (2.3 miles). The northbound Fretin chord – the deviation point for Paris to Lille trains – extends for 3.7 kilometres (2.3 miles) but here the line speed is only 220 km/h. There are four emergency loops – PRCI 14 Fresnoy, PRCI 23 Beugnatre, PRCI 27 Oignes, PRCI 30 Wannehain and PRCI 44 Hondeghem – located in open country. Except for Hondeghem which is 840 metres and can hold two Eurostar trainsets, the length of the other loops is 687 metres.

towards Lille. The classic line crosses TGV Nord Europe on the overbridge in the background. *Colin Marsden*

The Pas-de-Calais town Lens has daily TGV services to and from Paris Nord; Unit 511 is about to depart on a Dunkerque to Paris Nord service. *Colin Marsden*

To placate Arras and other towns not directly served by TGV Nord Europe, SNCF built a railhead station at Haute Picardie. Here passengers are joining a Sunday morning two-unit departure for Marseille and Montpellier. *Brian Perren*

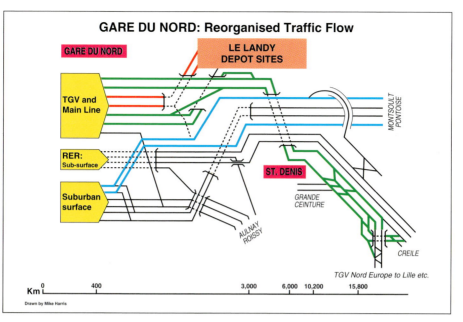

GARE DU NORD: Reorganised Traffic Flow

GARE DU NORD

LE LANDY DEPOT SITES

TGV and Main Line

RER: Sub-surface

Suburban surface

MONTSOULT PONTOISE

ST. DENIS

GRANDE CEINTURE

AULNAY ROISSY

CREILE

TGV Nord Europe to Lille etc.

Km | 0 | 400 | 3,000 | 6,000 | 10,200 | 15,800

Drawn by Mike Harris

Accès
C →

← Gare LILLE FLANDRES
LILLE FLANDRES station

↓ | Accès A | Accès B | Accès K | Accès L

Good design and clear signposting are features of TGV stations; this is Lille Europe. The sign directs customers to the nearby Lille Flandres station.
Brian Perren

TGV RHÔNE ALPES

SNCF's plans provide for the progressive extension of the original PSE line from a point north of Lyon – Montanay – to serve the Rhône Valley, Marseille, Nice, Montpellier and the Spanish border. The first stage of this plan – TGV Rhône Alpes from Montanay to St-Marcel-les-Valence – is now in service. Work on the next stage – TGV Méditerranée from Valence to Marseille/Montpellier – has started. Plans are being developed in conjunction with the Spanish to extend the line from Montpellier to the Spanish border. A plan to extend the high-speed line from the Marseille area through the Alpes Maritimes to the Côte d'Azur has been abandoned.

While the long-term objective is to extend the TGV to serve the South of France, the Rhône Alpes line has already brought a number of significant benefits to key points in the national network. Pressure on existing line capacity in the Lyon area – especially between Part-Dieu and Guillotière – has been eased. There is a new faster route for TGVs from Paris to Chambéry and Grenoble which has also eased pressure on the tortuous classic line from Mâcon via Ambérieu to Chambéry hitherto used by a number of TGVs. A new station has been built to serve Lyon's Satolas Airport. Government approval for the Rhône Alpes project was given in October 1987; Declaration of Public Utility was announced on 28 October 1989. The first stage – Montanay to St-Quentin-Fallavier – was opened on 13 December 1992 and the last stage from St-Quentin-Fallavier to St-Marcel-les-Valence on 3 July 1994. The cost of the line – which involved significant civil engineering – was FFR 7,267 million.

The Rhône Alpes route includes a number of viaducts and tunnels with 3.5% gradients. This picture of a two-unit PSE service shows the switchback characteristics of the line. *Brian Perren*

A number of spectacular tunnels and viaducts were necessary to take the TGV line through the challenging Rhône Alpes terrain. The 1,725-metre (1.1-mile) Viaduct De La Côtière takes the railway up to the tunnel on a 3.5% rising gradient. Line speed is 300 km/h. *SNCF-CAV*

Starting at Montanay (Km 380 on the original PSE line), the route of the 121-kilometre line was a compromise chosen to minimise environmental disturbance to a number of villages on the route and to cope with the demanding characteristics of the Rhône Alpes terrain. From Montanay the line initially heads to the east and then turns south near the village of Beynost, 11 kilometres from the start of the line. From Beynost, located on the plateau of La Dombes at an altitude of 320 metres, the line then has to descend for a distance of four kilometres to the level of the river Rhône at La Boisse, an altitude of 185 metres. This has entailed the construction of two tunnels – Des Dombes (500 metres) and La Côtière (291 metres) – followed immediately by the spectacular 1,725-metre (1.1 miles) Viaduct De La Côtière; the descent from Beynost to Km 15.6 (La Boisse) is 3.5%.

From the end of La Côtière viaduct the line runs alongside the A432 autoroute for a few kilometres as far as Satolas Airport TGV station, the layout of which consists of two loop platforms each with two faces and two centre tracks for non-stopping trains. Grenay, seven kilometres from Satolas, is the beginning of the series of junctions with the Lyon-Grenoble classic line. Extending for a distance of around eight kilometres, the grade-separated junctions consist of 160 km/h single-leads from the Paris direction which join the Grenoble line at St-Quentin-Fallavier and similar connections with the Lyon-Grenoble line towards the high-speed line in the direction of Valence.

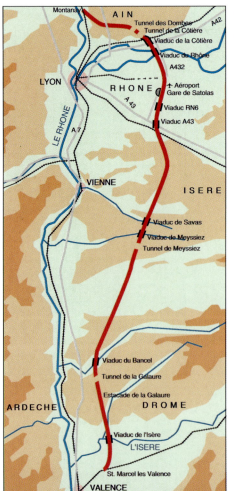

Left: Map of the Rhône Alpes line. *SNCF*

Facing page: Satolas TGV Station for Lyon International Airport was conceived as a long-term Rhône Alpes infrastructure enhancement. The pictures show various aspects of the striking award-winning design. PSE Unit 55 calls at the station to set down passengers from a Paris-Grenoble service. *Brian Perren*

Trains au Départ
Train Departures
Départ Destination   Particularités   Train   Voie

		TGV 904	4
GRENOBLE		TGV 905	3
LILLE EUROPE		TGV 520	4
		TGV 538	4

Porte RHONE   Porte ALPES

The Grenay-St-Marcel section of the line is characterised by the switchback nature of the route through the hills and valleys of the Rhône Alpes; there are three peaks each entailing 3.5% gradients in each direction. They are Diemoz (Km 45 – altitude 401 metres); Primarétte (Km 65 – altitude 471 metres and the highest point of the line); and St-Sorlin (Km 83 – altitude 327 metres). There are two tunnels – Meyssies (1,787 metres) and La Galaure (2,686 metres) – and several viaducts in this section.

Grenay – St-Quentin-Fallavier: the junction at Grenay – Km 417 on the Rhône Alpes line – enables TGVs from Paris to join the Lyon – Grenoble classic line and TGVs from Lyon to join the southbound high-speed line towards Valence. To maintain traffic flow, the junction layout has been designed with four single-lead chords, the geometry of which gives a line speed of 160 km/h (100 mph). The length of each chord is around 2 kilometres – a total of 8 kilometres or 5 track miles. Northbound TGVs from Grenoble (or Chambéry) to Paris and southbound TGVs from Lyon towards Valence can join the high-speed tracks at 160 km/h enabling a quick acceleration up to the 300 km/h line speed. Line speed for through trains is 300 km/h. The train is traversing the chord from the high-speed line towards Grenoble. *SNCF CAV*

Driver's view of the 3.5% rising gradient at Km 395 on the spectacular 1,725-metre (1.1-mile) Viaduct De La Côtière which carries the Rhône Alpes line up to the tunnel of the same name. *Brian Perren*

As the Rhône Alpes line will continue as TGV Méditerranée, the end of the line has been determined by the interface with the extension to the south. Thus, the end of the present route is at St-Marcel-les-Valence at a grade junction with the previously quiet non-electrified regional line from Valence to Grenoble; the junction is nine kilometres from Valence station on the classic PLM line to the South. This section of the line has been electrified at 25 kV to a point approaching Valence station where the power supplies change to the classic 1.5 kV for the PLM line.

Choosing an acceptable alignment for the Rhône Alpes line was a major challenge for the civil engineers. Given the topography of the Rhône Alpes region – in particular the 130-metre difference in levels between the hills of La Côtière and the valley of the River Rhône and the hills forming the Bas Dauphiné to the south of the route – the rising gradient had to be 3.5% approaching the four peak points on the line. The route has a total of 138 bridges – 63 road, 73 rail and two major rail grade separations. The most interesting features are the four tunnels which total 5,246 metres (3.25 miles). To allow trains to pass at 300 km/h – a combined speed of 600 km/h – these huge tunnels have been built to a height which allows free air space of 100 cubic metres. The ends of the tunnels are built to facilitate the release of air compressed by the entry of a TGV, thus minimising the effect of pressure waves on the ears.

TGV Rhône Alpes is signalled for full bi-directional working at 300 km/h with crossovers at strategic points. There are three emergency sidings. Given the number of short 3.5% gradients and the need to maintain an even flow of traffic on a four-minute headway at 300 km/h, the section of line between Grenay and St-Marcel is signalled with TVM 430; Grenay to Montanay is signalled with the older TVM 300.

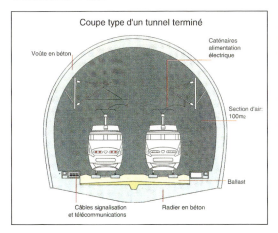

Coupe type d'un tunnel terminé

Voûte en béton

Caténaires alimentation électrique

Section d'air: 100m2

Ballast

Câbles signalisation et télécommunications

Radier en béton

To allow two trains to pass at 300 km/h tunnels on the Rhône Alpes line have been built with 100 square metres of free air space. *SNCF*

Moisenay is the point where the original Paris Sud Est line joins the north end of the Rhône Alpes extension. The Atlantique set on the left of the picture has come from Lyon and is bound for Paris. The line on the right-hand side of the picture is the re-aligned southbound track towards Lyon; the re-alignment necessitated a reduced speed of 220 km/h, but deceleration is necessary as this location is towards the end of the Paris Sud Est line. *Brian Perren*

To accommodate the connecting lines from La Jonction – shown passing over this southbound chord of the re-aligned Paris Sud Est line – the layout at Crisenoy was remodelled. Southbound PSE unit bound for Lyon. *Brian Perren*

LA JONCTION EN ILE-DE-FRANCE

Because of its geography and population distribution, most major road and rail links in France tended to radiate from Paris – but over two-thirds of journeys by all transport modes are made from province-to-province. Cross-country rail journeys were often slow and in many cases it was quicker to travel via Paris, even though the distance was longer and it might entail changing terminal stations. It is for these reasons that SNCF's share of the cross-country market has been negligible.

Nonetheless, as business on the Paris-Lyon TGV service began to grow research showed that significant numbers of passengers who had joined trains at the Gare-de-Lyon had started their journeys from places as far away as Lille in the north. There was also significant business from Rouen and the western suburbs of Paris such as Mantes-la-Jolie and Versailles. To develop this traffic SNCF launched a direct TGV service from Lille to Lyon which by-passed Paris by using a series of freight lines which circle the city known as the 'Grande Ceinture'. Introduced in September 1984, the Lille to Lyon TGV soon built up custom to the extent that a second service was added, plus a similar service to Rouen which also served Mantes-la-Jolie and Versailles.

Given the substantial journey time reductions which TGV can offer it was clear that, providing a means of linking the main TGV routes out of Paris could be organised, competitive journey times between the major French centres could be substantially reduced to levels within – or close to – the three-hour threshold at which point air starts to become quicker than rail overall. Lille to Lyon is the prime opportunity. So far as leisure travel is concerned, the times by cross-country TGVs would be far quicker than could ever be achieved by private car. To develop the tremendous potential for direct province-to-province traffic – plus international business by TGV Nord Europe from the UK, Belgium, the Netherlands and Germany – SNCF prepared plans for a high-speed route to the east of Paris which would link the Nord Europe, Atlantique and Paris Sud Est lines. In October 1987 the government approved the construction of the new line; the route was agreed in February 1988 and the Declaration of Public Utility was obtained in June 1990. Variously described as the Paris Interconnexion, TGV Ile-de-France, but now generally referred to as La Jonction, the north-south section was opened in May 1994; the west branch was opened in June 1996. The line will also connect with TGV Est Européen when this is built. As can be seen from the map on page 36, and as explained earlier, La Jonction Oeust (West) is in effect an extension of the PSE line on a more favourable alignment to Créteil, a point much closer to the centre of Paris. This has released capacity on the PLM between Créteil and Lieusaint for longer-distance commuter and freight traffic.

There is another important reason for La Jonction – improvement of access for the growing number of people now living in the expanding Ile-de-France region. Increasing centres of activity such as business and large schools are being built outside Paris and located near good trunk roads. Massy in the west, Marne-la-Vallée in the east and Roissy are now large centres of activity, and others are planned. All of these need good rail access. The Réseau Express Regional (RER) Paris outer-urban rapid transit system has already been extended to serve these new developments. To serve these centres there are three major interchange stations – Massy, Marne-la-Vallée-Chessy and Aéroport Charles De Gaulle – in the Ile-de-France Region. Each has ample car parking, bus services, RER and a TGV station.

Comprising 102 kilometres (63 miles) of route, La Jonction starts on a triangular junc-

Located on La Jonction line, Marne-le-Vallée-Chessey station – which also serves Disneyland Paris – is served by Eurostar, THALYS and many SNCF domestic TGVs. *SNCF/CAV*

tion with the Nord Europe line at Vémars, from where it heads south to the first station – Aéroport Charles De Gaulle TGV (Roissy) – seven kilometres from Vémars. Developed in association with *Aéroports de Paris and the Conseil Regional Ile-de-France*, Paris Airport is a major multi-modal interchange. In addition to the TGV station – which has two through tracks and four platforms loops – RER Line B has been extended from the old rather inconvenient terminal to the new station. A spectacular four-level interchange module has been built above the sub-surface TGV station which also provides access between the four sub-terminals which form airport Terminal 2. This building consists of two round 350-metre sections, above which is a four-star hotel.

Beyond Roissy the line heads south east to the second station – Marne-La-Vallée-Chessy – 31 kilometres (19.26 miles) from Vémars. As well as providing access for this large new town development, Marne-la-Vallée station – which is also the terminus for RER Line A – is located next to the Disneyland Paris leisure park. The Disneyland Paris company contributed to the cost of the station which consists of two through tracks on the outside of the station and three platform roads in the centre. There are three stabling sidings to hold special trains which can be run for Disneyland visitors. Between Marne-La-Vallée and Bussy St-George, where the line crosses the A4 Autoroute, the Jonction line is around 30 kilometres to the east of the centre of Paris.

From Marne-la-Vallée the line continues for 20 or so kilometres (12.4 miles) through open country to the series of junctions forming the Coubert triangle providing the following routeings – Nord Europe to Paris Sud Est, Nord Europe to Atlantique, Paris Sud Est to Atlantique and Paris Sud Est to Gare-de-Lyon.

As most of the trains passing through the Coubert layout will be between the Gare-de-Lyon and South East France, the south-to-west side of the triangle is the main route; the north-to-south and north-west chords are the connecting junctions. At Crisenoy, 14 kilometres from Coubert and 69 kilometres from the Nord Europe junction at Vémars, the Jonction joins the Paris Sud Est line, 17 kilometres from the start of the original PSE alignment at Lieusaint.

From Coubert the 26-kilometre (16-mile) west branch (Jonction Ouest) passes through open country near Brie-Comte-Robert before reaching the outskirts of the Paris residential area. To provide environmental protection in these sensitive areas the line passes through a 2,199-metre (1.4-mile) covered section at Villecrenses followed by a 1,635-metre (1-mile) tunnel at Limeil-Brévannes. Just beyond the tunnel, at Valenton, there is a grade-separated junction – Bifurcation Massy – with the Grande Ceinture freight line, reference to which was made earlier. As it is not cost-effective to upgrade or build new infrastructure in this part of the Paris area, for the present TGVs bound for the Atlantique line will use Grande Ceinture tracks as far as Massy. Just beyond the Valenton junction, the Jonction Ouest – which is also the PSE line into Paris – joins the classic PLM line on a grade-separated junction at Créteil, nine kilometres (5.6 miles) from the Gare-de-Lyon terminal station.

Given the requirement for stations at both Roissy Airport and Marne-La-Vallée – plus the need to avoid residential areas, recreation areas and sensitive nature locations such as the Ferrières forest – an acceptable route for the north-south leg of the Jonction involved some constraints. Thus, the alignment was designed for a minimum-radius curve of 4,200 metres compared with 5,000 metres on the Nord Europe and other routes; consequently the maximum line speed is 270 km/h (167.8 mph). For some sections – Vémars to Roissy – and over the north-south chord at Coubert, the maximum speed is 230 km/h. As most services call at Roissy Airport and commence deceleration several kilometres before the station, the reduced line speed here is to some extent academic. The line is signalled for full two-way working at maximum line speed in each direction. There are numerous crossovers throughout the route. TVM430 cab-signalling applies between Vémars and the north side of the Coubert triangle where the signalling is TVM300. Operating headway is four minutes. Formation width is 13.6 metres with a 4.2-metre distance between track centres; these dimensions reflect the 270 km/h line speed on this route. Power supplies are 25kV.

From the start of Jonction Oeust at Créteil and from the spur line from the Grande Ceinture at Valenton (Massy Junction), power supply is 1.5kV dc and the signalling is classic lateral; line speed is 160 km/h. Power supply changeover to 25kV ac is just beyond Massy Junction. Near Yerres (seven kilometres from Créteil) lateral signalling is replaced by TVM300 and the line speed is raised from 160 to 270 km/h. Because the PSE line is equipped with TVM300 and as a significant number of PSE and almost all Atlantique trainsets have only TVM300 on-board equipment, it was preferable to signal the Jonction Oeust through to the interface with the Sud Est line at Crisenoy with TVM300. The distance from Créteil to Crisenoy via Jonction Oeust is 2.7 kilometres more than the original route through Lieusaint, but line speeds are higher, giving a small reduction of journey time.

LA JONCTION RAILHEAD STATIONS			
	Aéroport Charles de Gaulle TGV	Mame La Vallée-Chessy	Massy TGV
Opened	13 November 1994	29 May 1994	29 September 1991
Cost	Francs 1,320 m (1989 values)	Francs 830 m (1989 values)	Francs 195 m (1986 values)
Estimated passengers per year	900,000	540,000	520,000
TGVs per day	36	32	22
Parking	700	800	800
RER	B	A	B and C
Buses	Airport and local	Local services	Local plus RATP

THE BELGIAN HIGH-SPEED LINES

Plans for the Belgian high-speed line were first tabled in 1985 when the decision to build the Channel Tunnel was made. At the end of 1988 the transport ministers of the countries involved with the European high-speed rail network agreed that 15 May 1993 – one of the several target dates for the opening of the Channel Tunnel – would also be the target for completing the associated infrastructure in France and Belgium. Despite its importance as a key link in the European high-speed network, the first short section of the Belgian line – 14 kilometres from the French Frontier to Antoing – did not open until 2 June 1996.

These delays had their roots in the on-going rivalry between the Walloon and Flemish factions of Belgian society who could not agree on the choice of route; organising funding was also a problem. Even though an acceptable route was eventually agreed in July 1991, the start of the work was further delayed by negotiations for planning permission for a number of works on the line of route. The next section from Antoing to the approaches to Brussels Midi opened December 1997.

Belgium's TGV line – which is Y-shaped – consists of 88 kilometres (55 miles) from the French Frontier to Brussels Midi, of which 71 kilometres from the frontier to Lembeek is new construction and 17 kilometres of upgraded infrastructure from Lembeek to Brussels Midi; 87 kilometres (54 miles), of which 47 kilometres is upgraded infrastructure, from Brussels to Antwerp, and 40 kilometres of new construction from Antwerp to the Netherlands Border; and 146 kilometres (91 miles) of part-new and part-upgraded infrastructure from Brussels to the German border.

The stem of the Y is the interface with SNCF TGV Nord Europe at Wannehain – the France-Belgium frontier some 11 kilometres (6.2 miles) to the east of the triangular junction at Fretin. There is no frontier post at Wannehain and where the tracks cross the border TGV Nord Europe becomes the Belgian high-speed line.

The South section route is to the south of Tournai. There is a short 356-metre cut-and-cover section to protect the village of Bruyelle and a 438-metre viaduct to carry the railway over the Escaut River before the line reaches Antoing. At Antoing there is a 160 km/h single-lead junction with the classic SNCB line from Mouscron to Mons, Charleroi and Liège. Until December 1997 this junction was the route for the Paris-Brussels/Amsterdam/THALYS service.

From Antoing the route is through open country to a point to the south of the town of Ath, 38 kilometres from Wannehain and 50 kilometres from Brussels Midi. Near Ath is the imposing 2,005-metre Arbre Viaduct – likely to be one of the longest railway viaducts in Europe – which straddles the villages of Ath and Chièvres. The choice of the Arbre Viaduct was conditioned by the need to cross the Ath-Blaton Canal, the eastern half of the River Dendre, the Mons road and the Ath-Jurbise railway.

For the next 12 kilometres from Ath the new route is alongside the existing Tournai-Brussels line as far as Silly, where there are two single-track connections – one from (Km 41) and one to Brussels (Km 44). Now the line parallels the Autoroute A8 for a few kilometres passing Tubize to reach Lembeek from where it is again alongside existing infrastructure, the Mons-Brussels Line 96. At Halle, already a major railway location, the layout has been enhanced with new railway bridges and a cut-and-cover section; at Lembeek power supplies change from 25 kV, which has been adopted for the new TGV line, to 3 kV for the ensuing 17 kilometres into Brussels Midi.

The modernised terminal area at Brussels Midi. *SNCB/NNBS*

This last 17-kilometre section of route to Brussels Midi involves the expansion of the existing infrastructure from two to four tracks; two tracks will be used by high-speed trains at a maximum speed of 220 km/h. This involves major works, especially the construction of new flyovers, at Lembeek, Lot, Forest and Brussels. Brussels Midi terminal station has been comprehensively remodelled both for the introduction of THALYS TGVs from Paris and Eurostar trains from London. Eurostar has two dedicated platforms – Nos 1 and 2 – with other TGV services using platforms 3 to 6.

Technical characteristics of the Wannehain-Brussels section are similar to TGV Nord Europe. Maximum speed between Wannehain and Tubize is 300 km/h, although the alignment is suitable for 330 km/h which may be permitted at a later date; maximum speed from Tubize to Brussels Midi is 220 km/h. Changeover from 25 kV ac power supplies to the standard SNCB 3kV dc and from TVM430 cab-signalling to SNCB ATBL cab-signalling will be made on the move at Tubize/Lembeek. With some exceptions, minimum radius curves will normally be 6,000 metres; maximum gradient is 2% (1 in 50). Distance between track centres is 4.5 metres.

At Schaarbeek, the first station after Brussels Noord, the TGV line will divide into two separate routes forming the two prongs of the Y mentioned earlier. The north fork will be the existing route to Antwerp and the Netherlands border, but upgraded and vastly improved although limited to a maximum speed of 160 km/h. Antwerp Central station – which is a dead-end terminal – and its associated track layout will be transformed. A new sub-surface station for TGVs and other international trains will be built. The capacity of Antwerp Central station – considered to be the constraining bottleneck of the entire SNCB system – will be doubled.

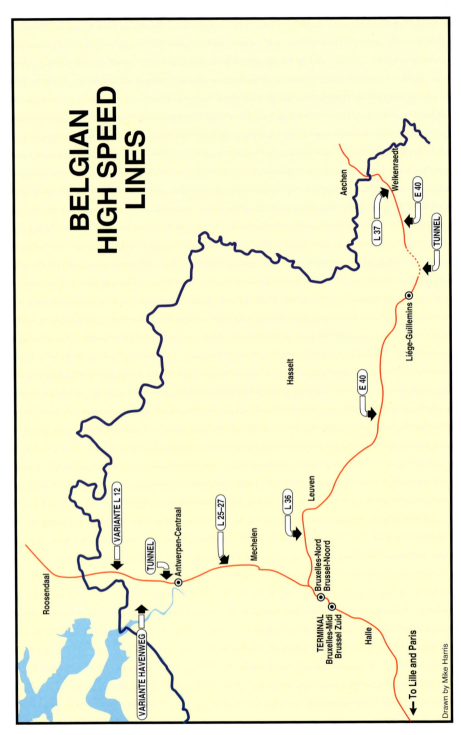

BELGIAN
HIGH SPEED
LINES

Roosendaal

VARIANTE L 12

TUNNEL

Antwerpen-Centraal

VARIANTE HAVENWEG

L 25–27

Mechelen

L 36

Leuven

Bruxelles-Nord
Brussel-Noord

TERMINAL
Bruxelles-Midi
Brussel Zuid

Halle

→ To Lille and Paris

Hasselt

E 40

Lége-Guillemins

Aechen

L 37

Welkenraedt

E 40

TUNNEL

Drawn by Mike Harris

The choice of route northwards from Antwerp has been the subject of much discussion between the Belgian and Netherlands governments. Although the location for the link-up between the Netherlands South high-speed line and the northwards extension of TGV Belge have now been agreed, the Belgian government originally preferred a different alignment. Heading north from Antwerp the Belgians favoured either upgrading the existing international route through Roosendaal or a new line starting near the Antwerp dock area and crossing into the Netherlands at Zandvliet. The route through the dock area would have minimised environmental impact in Belgium. Even though there are similarly sensitive environmental issues in the Netherlands, given the importance of Breda as a generator of traffic both to Rotterdam and Antwerp, the Netherlands' preferred choice of an easterly alignment was accepted by the Belgians, although this entails some 16 kilometres of additional route construction on the Belgian side of the frontier. The Netherlands Government will compensate the Belgian Government for this extra investment. The distance from Antwerp Central station to the beginning of the new infrastructure is five kilometres and the distance from here to the Netherlands Frontier is 35 kilometres.

Starting at Schaarbeek the East route is through Leuven, Liège, Aachen to the German Frontier. The first 30 kilometres is existing infrastructure, which will be widened to four tracks and upgraded to 200 km/h. There will be a short 160 km/h section where the route passes through the existing station at Leuven, and then a short tunnel under the E40 autoroute. The next 60 kilometres will be a new 300 km/h alignment alongside the E40, which will give a journey time of 39 minutes for the 106 kilometres between Brussels and Liège. The line will also be used by 200 km/h domestic inter-city trains as well as THALYS services.

The next 43 kilometres from Liège to Aachen passes under heavy terrain through a 6.5-kilometre tunnel. After the tunnel the new line will rejoin the E40 autoroute alignment as far as Welkenraedt. Here, where THALYS services into and out of Germany will rejoin the existing route to obtain access to the existing Aachen station, plans are being developed for upgrading the cross-border section of the present line for 160 km/h and the design for a new viaduct at Hammersbruck. On the other side of the border, part of the line has a permanent restriction of 40 km/h, but the German railway has plans to upgrade this section for 120 km/h.

Although the Wannehain-Brussel Midi section is now open, funding for the North (Netherlands) and East (German) sections is much more difficult. Given the expected traffic volumes from Paris and London to Brussels, the rate of return for the South section is expected to be a satisfactory 8%. Unfortunately, the traffic projections for the North and East sections totals only five million passengers per year on each leg, which is not enough to cover the cost of construction. Nevertheless, despite the poor commercial prospects, the Belgian government has signed agreements with neighbouring countries and its own regional authorities committing it to construct the international high-speed line from frontier to frontier.

So far the Belgian government has agreed to pay a share of the infrastructure costs equivalent to the use made by upgraded sections of line by Belgian domestic trains. A small subsidy was promised by the European Union to cover some interest charges, but this was not sufficient to bring the rate of return up to an acceptable level. An application for additional EU funding led to a priority ranking for the project in the Trans European Network programme and it is hoped that this will lead to an allocation of additional subsidies allowing the project to continue.

Assuming sufficient funding can be organised, the North section should be complete by 2005 while the Eastern section will be phased-in in stages between 2002 and 2005.

THE PARIS SUD EST FLEET

At an early stage in TGV development gas turbine propulsion was seriously considered as the choice of traction. Although on the face of things electricity was the obvious means of powering the new trains, there were lingering doubts about the efficiency of current collection from the overhead catenary at very high speeds. Consequently, SNCF undertook more research into the problems of current collection when dual-voltage locomotive CC 21001 was tested up to 283 km/h (167 mph) in ac mode between Strasbourg and Mulhouse in Alsace. Further study of the issues – and the decision of the French government to build a national network of nuclear-powered electricity generating stations – led SNCF to opt for electric traction for TGV and classic routes with appropriate levels of traffic. A high-speed gas-turbine set was built and, together with a single unit electric car, was used as a test-bed for the development of the new generation of TGV trains.

Given that the new TGV train service timetables would combine high-speed, high frequency and more intensive trainset utilisation, SNCF chose fixed-formation rather than separate locomotives and coaches for the new Paris Sud Est railway. Four basic design rules were set for the new trains and have been perpetuated for all subsequent TGV builds. They are: fixed-formation trainsets; articulated configuration for the passenger coaches; body rather than bogie-mounted traction motors; and to minimise track wear a maximum axle-load of 17 tonnes. Articulation was chosen to allow low-slung bodies to be carried on a reduced number of bogies thereby saving weight, reducing drag and minimising energy consumption and also enhancing passenger comfort by obviating the need for seats to be positioned over the bogies. It is also easier to gain access to low-slung vehicles. With the vehicle ends mounted over the bogies, a spacious vestibule area was designed which is tightly sealed to ensure the highest standards of sound insulation and air-conditioning.

Each PSE trainset consists of two power cars (M1 and M2) enclosing eight articulated trailers R1 to R8. This SNCF vehicle identification is based on M for *motrice* and R for *remorque*, the English terms for which are power car and trailer car. To provide sufficient power to sustain speeds up to 270 km/h (167.8 mph) and to cope with 3.5% gradients, the designers required a power output of around 6,000 kW. If motors large enough to provide this output were only carried on the two power cars, the axle-load would be too great and would exceed the 17-tonne maximum stipulation. Consequently, the PSE sets have 12 537 kW traction motors totalling 6,450 kV carried on six motor bogies, four of which are positioned on the two power cars and two under the outer ends of R1 and R8 adjoining the power cars.

Like recent electrification projects the new *lignes à grande vitesse* have 25 kV ac power supplies. However, because significant sections of the SNCF network are electrified at 1.5 kV dc and the cost of converting to the more efficient 25 kV ac is not a practical proposition, the TGV – like most contemporary SNCF locomotives and power cars – is equipped for dual-voltage operation. When operating in ac mode a single pantograph is used for current collection; power to supply the other traction motors at the opposite end of the rake is carried along a 25 kV line along the roof of each unit. In dc mode two separate dc pantographs are used with power supplied direct to the traction motors.

Trainset bodies are formed from a tubular girder structure, plated in semi-stainless steel, glass and polyester. A classic coupler is used between the power cars and R1 and R8 and there is a Scharfenberg auto-coupler enabling two trainsets to be joined to operate as a multiple-unit. The air-conditioned driving cab includes a number of modern driving and safety aids including a speed selection device, anti-skid device, inter-phone for communication with other train staff, radio link with centralised train control centre and TVM cab-signalling.

Left: Awaiting departure from Lausanne to Paris, this is the first of the nine 3-voltage France-Suisse sets to receive the new livery and La Ligne de Coeur route branding. *Brian Perren*

Below: Until all PSE sets are repainted in the new blue-grey standard TGV livery, there will be occasions when two PSE units carrying the old and new livery will be used for a two-unit service. This two-unit Annecy to Paris via Chambéry train is leaving Aix-les-Bains. *Brian Perren*

When they first entered service the PSE units were equipped with classic primary suspension by rubber studs and spiral springs, but this was subsequently replaced by SR10 air suspension. Equipped with rheostatic braking, each bogie brake is independent of the others and there is a high-power electro-pneumatic air brake. Double cast iron shoes are on all wheels and two double discs on each carrying axle.

Trainset length is 200.190 metres. Power cars are 22.150 metres, the two motor-trailers R1 and R8 are 21.845 metres and each trailer R2 to R7 is 18.700 metres. Bogie length – power cars and trailers – is 3 metres, wheel diameters are 0.920 metres. Mass is 385 tonnes. Power-to-weight ratio is 16.75 kW or 22.46 hp per tonne.

There have been a number of changes in the composition of the original PSE fleet since the trains first entered service a couple of years before the first stage of the PSE was inaugurated in September 1981. A total of 111½ trainsets were built in four basic versions – two-voltage two-class; three-voltage two-class; two-voltage first class; and the trainsets built to carry mail for PTT, the French Post Office. During the next few years – as trainsets become due for mid-life refurbishment and in response to market and technical developments – there will be different sub-series versions.

Originally there were 92 two-voltage two-class and eight two-class sets equipped with a third voltage 15 kV 16 2/3Hz ac power supplies for running over Swiss tracks to Lausanne and Bern. Power supplies over the 15 km section of route from the French border crossing at La Plaine to Geneva Cornavin station are basic SNCF 1.5 kV dc. One two-voltage two-class set has been withdrawn following collision damage and another, Unit 88, following extensive use as a test train for synchronous traction motors, has been modified to three-voltage to strengthen the Swiss sub-fleet and renumbered 118. In another development, Unit 114 has been sold by SNCF to Swiss Railways (SBB) to capitalise the SBB involvement in the jointly-managed France-Swiss TGV service.

Over the years a number of changes have been made to the two-class two-voltage fleet. Following extensive in-service experience a programme of internal modifications was undertaken. The original bar space, which was far too small and cramped, was extended by removing two bays of second class seats in R4 and the seating in first class car R1 has been modified to provide more space for meal service, reducing the total number of seats in the train from 386 to 368. Telephones were also installed.

In 1993 SNCF started an on-going programme of PSE modifications. To enable PSE trains to run over the Grenay – St Marcel-les-Valence section of the Rhône Alpes line which is signalled with TVM 430, a number of two-voltage two-class sets had their TVM 300 equipment replaced by the new system. Next, in preparation for a more comprehensive mid-life refurbishment programme, two pre-series trains – one technical and one commercial – were prepared at Bisheim Works. Technical conversion of Unit 87 – which is part of the PSE route improvement programme – includes re-gearing the traction motors and enhancing the braking performance so that the maximum speed can be raised from 270 to 300 km/h. TVM 430 will be fitted to those trains not equipped under the interim project.

Although the trains were comfortable, the original decor of the PSE fleet – which in some ways resembles the mid-1970s Corail coaches – was functional and in some respects spartan, and now compares unfavourably with the latest Atlantique, Réseau and Duplex trains. Consequently, it was agreed that a complete refurbishment of both the interior and the exterior of the PSE trains would be implemented as part of the major mid-life refurbishment, the date for which was now approaching for earlier units in the build. Unit 98 was selected for pre-series passenger evaluation. Six of its eight coaches were given a major facelift with new décor, new seating and improved buffet area, the style of which is based on the latest Réseau design. It was also decided to replace the original orange external livery and repaint the train in the blue-grey now adopted for the Atlantique, Réseau and Duplex trains. Technical and general refurbishment of 30 trains is now in progress. Several sets were in service by the end of 1996, and these will be followed by 13/14 trains per year from January 1997 to December 1998. Apart from the power-car styling, the trains now look very similar to the latest Réseau series. Because of the more generous second class seat-pitch, the number of seats has been reduced from 386 in the original 1981 version to 350 in the 1996 refurbished version.

Except for the seating layout – 285 instead of 368 places in the two-class PSEs – the first class sets are identical to the two-class version. These trains were acquired to cope with business travellers on peak trains between Paris and Lyon, and subsequently to Grenoble. While they were a useful facility, they could not be used effectively on other services and consequently were under-utilised compared with the rest of the PSE fleet. SNCF now believes that the new double-deck Duplex trains – which have 197 compared with 108 first class seats in a PSE two-class trainset – will be sufficient to cope with busy peak-services between Paris and Lyon. One unit – No. 38 – has been withdrawn and converted into an additional postal train; others will be incorporated into the two-class refurbishment programme. One set is to be used to test tilting (pendular) technology for both classic and TGV purposes.

Recognising the value of a high-speed train which could carry post traffic, PTT – the French postal service – funded the purchase of 2½ trainsets for use between postal stations at Paris, Mâcon and Lyon. Technically the trains are identical to the passenger sets, but there are no windows; the space is used for the stowage of trolleys conveying sacks of mail. Access is through the door in the side of each vehicle. Two sets were used to cover the original service with one half-set as spare to cover maintenance periods. As the PTT sets have the same configuration as the rest of the fleet – two power cars and eight articulated trailers – the spare half-set has to be lifted off its bogies to be marshalled into the train.

With the opening of the Rhône Alpes line in 1994, the PTT extended its rail network and opened a new depot at Cavaillon in Provence. As it was not possible to cover the new service with only 2½ trainsets, SNCF made available first class Unit 38 which was converted to a postal train at Bisheim Works; the set is identical to the other postal trains. To work on the Rhône Alpes line, all postal trains have been equipped with TVM 430 cab-signalling and are likely to be upgraded for 300 km/h sometime in the future.

To formalise its stake in the France-Suisse GIE, Swiss Railways (SBB) has purchased PSE Unit 112 which now carries the logo of its Swiss owners. All nine PSE three-voltage 'Swiss' units are to be refurbished and repainted; this will include the new route logo and styling.
Michael J Collins

Accommodation in the first PSE series was somewhat austere. To bring these older trains up to the standards of ambience now enjoyed in the latest Réseau fleet, SNCF has undertaken a long-term programme of refurbishment. These pictures show the original first class accommodation; first class upgraded to the latest Réseau standards; and second class upgraded to the latest Réseau standards. Internally the refurbished PSE and latest Réseau sets are almost identical.
SNCF Jaspaud Desgraupes

THE ATLANTIQUE FLEET

By the time a firm order was placed with Alsthom in November 1985 to build 95 Atlantique trainsets – subsequently increased by 10 to a total of 105 – SNCF had accumulated four years' technical and commercial experience of operating train services at speeds up to 270 km/h with the PSE fleet. In addition to this day-to-day experience, SNCF – in close association with Alsthom – had initiated a number of technical development programmes with particular regard to riding qualities at even higher speeds, traction motor development and the use of microprocessor technology for a range of operating aids.

Highlight of these tests was a new world speed record of 380 km/h (236 mph) – subsequently bettered in 1990 – with PSE Unit 16 on 27 September 1981. This research produced two important technical developments – the decision to use SR 10 air suspension and synchronous traction motors in the Atlantique design. Surprisingly, despite the excellent performance of air suspension on other contemporary European rolling stock including its own Corail coaches, SNCF at first chose heliocoidal springing for the PSE secondary suspension. Following the satisfactory outcome of tests, SNCF decided to retrofit the PSE fleet with SR 10 air suspension.

Pending delivery of Réseau units, Atlantique sets were used for Paris Sud Est routes. This morning service from Geneva to Paris slows for the curve at Culoz. *Brian Perren*

Atlantique driving cab. In later TGV derivatives the driver's position has been moved from the left to the centre of the cab to give better vision and provide space for the growing number of cab-signalling systems necessary for international working. *GEC Alsthom*

The most important feature of the Atlantique train is the self-commutating three-phase ac synchronous traction motor. Not only does the synchronous (or commutatorless) motor provide more power per weight and volume than a conventional dc motor, but its maintenance costs are very much lower. The commutators on the PSE dc traction motors have to be reprofiled every 300,000 or so kilometres (186,420 miles). Whereas a PSE trainset needs twelve 537 kW motors to meet its performance specification, the Atlantique train can function with eight similar size synchronous traction motors each with an output of 1,100 kW. With 8,800 kW – but also allowing that the maximum gradients on the Atlantique line are much less demanding than the PSE – it was possible to add two extra trailers as well as raising the maximum speed to 300 km/h (186 mph). With eight instead of 12 traction motors, only four motor bogies instead of six are required, obviating the need for equipment to be located at the outer end of R1 and R10 trailers.

To cope with 300 km/h two other technical features were incorporated into the Atlantique design – new pantographs and braking system. To ensure efficient current collection at 300 km/h on the Atlantique line and speeds of up to 220 km/h (137 mph) on those parts of the classic line (Tours to Bordeaux) where dc current has to be taken from old pre-World War 2 catenary, a new pantograph – the GPU – was designed. This has a unique large plunger with a second stage which has also been redesigned. The new design has been used for the dc as well as the ac pantographs; on classic track in dc mode two pantographs are used. The new braking system makes use of high powered non-ventilated disc brakes in combination with a microprocessor controlled anti-skid device.

Equally important is the application of microprocessor systems both on board the Atlantique train and at maintenance depots and control centres. In the 10 or so years since the PSE train was designed, both the number and sophistication of computers available on the market has enabled development of advanced communication technology for rail purposes. It is now possible to use microprocessors for a range of diverse functions including anything from control of wheel slip, brake monitoring, control of air-conditioning, door closing and the provision of on-board passenger information displays.

Known as 'Tornad', the Atlantique computer network is an on-board data system built around inter-related microprocessors positioned throughout the train. The centrepiece is the two computers located in the driver's cab. These control a range of functions including pre-test of equipment prior to departure, the trouble-shooting guide for the driver to quickly locate and rectify any malfunction, monitoring of the braking system both prior to departure and on the move and control of the public address system.

Thanks to the radio link, the great benefit of 'Tornad' is the ability to transmit data from the train to the shore and vice versa. For example, not only is the driver warned of any equipment malfunction by reference to the VDU on his cab console, but the fault is retained in the unit's maintenance log book in Châtillon Depot. So at the end of each day's working, the depot has a complete list of faults on every unit before it arrives. This enables the depot to plan the workload and organise the replacement of any spare parts which may be necessary. Another feature enables the depot supervisor to switch on the air-conditioning remotely from his office instead of having to go out to the train – clearly a new-era of rail maintenance technology.

While the appearance and outward profile of the Atlantique trains shows a strong family resemblance to its PSE predecessors, the profile on the higher point of the two power cars has been realigned to give a more integrated roof line. To ensure that the trains were seen as second-generation TGVs, the red-orange finish used on the PSEs was replaced by a new silver-white and blue finish. Sliding plug door panels are painted red for first class, yellow for the bar car and green for second class. These new technical improvements reduced current consumption to a significant extent.

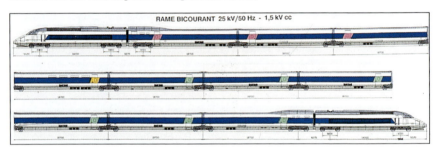

Atlantique trainset configuration. *SNCF*

While the sophisticated engineering innovations will be of considerable interest to the connoisseurs of rail traction technology, the internal design improvements and new range of on-board amenities are more readily apparent to SNCF's customers. At the time that the PSE trains were designed, SNCF had started to move away from the luxury market as exemplified by equipment built for the Paris-Brussels, Paris-Nice (Mistral), and Paris-Bordeaux TEEs, and had narrowed its focus towards journey-time reductions and standards of quality aimed to meet the needs of a wider market. At that time, it was envisaged that most TGV journeys would be within the 2fi to 3-hour journey-time band and it was only later that longer journeys were contemplated. Accordingly, the initial layout of the PSE train was comfortable but relatively simple.

Partly because average journeys on the Atlantique network are longer but also because rail has to maintain its competitive edge vis-à-vis other transport modes, an imaginative range of on-board facilities was incorporated into the Atlantique design. There are three first class, six second class and a bar/lounge car: a total of 485 seats. The set is numbered M1, R1 to R10, and M2. A welcome improvement is that an entire coach (R4) is used for a catering and lounge area, not just as a place to buy drinks and snacks but as a place to linger and socialise; the bar area also includes a gift and magazine shop.

As the Atlantique sets only have four motor bogies compared with six in the PSE sets, the space at the outer ends of R1 and R10 is not needed to house an additional motor block and has been used for passenger accommodation. At the first class end (vehicle R1) the space has been used to create a small but stylish conference *salon* with video facilities which can be reserved by businessmen travelling in groups who wish to use the journey time for business meetings. At the opposite end of the rake R10 has been used to provide an *espace enfants* young persons' area. A completely new design concept has been applied to the first class accommodation. Coach R1, which is next to the power car, is a standard open plan coach with face-to-face seating at tables; there is a facility in this coach for a handicapped traveller with wheelchair. Seating in R1 is designated 'Coach'.

Atlantique First Class 'Club' seating. *SNCF*

In the other two first class coaches – designated 'Club' – the layout is striking and very stylish. On one side of the centre aisle the seating is standard open plan with two face-to-face seats and tables; on the opposite side of the aisle the seating is in groups of four face-to-face with tables but in semi-compartment layout. First class passengers have the choice of three styles of seating: 'Coach', 'Club' duo or quatro, and the *salon*. At-seat meal service is supplied from a galley between coaches R1 and R2. All toilets are retention type and there are three telephone cabins in the train.

Seating configuration in second class is a mixture of uni-directional and facing. A useful facility has been provided at the adjoining ends of coaches R8 and R9 where the seating has been designed for families travelling in groups of two to five people; a fifth sideways seat has been fitted between the normal pairs of facing seats. A special nursery toilet is installed in R8 for the two family areas.

At first the Atlantique fleet was deployed exclusively on services from Paris Montparnasse to the west and south west of France. Subsequently, a small number were used to strengthen the PSE fleet for services from the Gare-de-Lyon including Geneva, Annecy and Grenoble. However, because of their increased length maintenance can only be undertaken at the Châtillon facility involving a circuitous journey to and from the Gare-de-Lyon every two or so days.

Atlantique sets are also used for cross-country services from Poitiers, Nantes and Rennes to Lyon and from Bordeaux to Lille Europe. Twenty sets have been fitted with TVM 430 for working over the Nord Europe line to Lille Europe; this facility will also enable Atlantique sets to operate over the Rhône Alpes line to the South of France if required.

THE RÉSEAU FLEET

While the first and second generation trainsets were designed to meet the particular characteristics of the Paris Sud Est and Atlantique routes, with the opening of La Jonction in 1994 TGV journeys could now be much longer – nine-and-a-half hours from Brussels Midi to Nice is a case in point. For these inter-réseau services between the Nord, Sud Est and Atlantique lines, and also to provide extra capacity on the PSE line, where journey lengths have also been increased, SNCF placed orders with GEC Alsthom in January 1990 for a build of 90 'universal' trains designated TGV Réseau (TGV-R). It was originally intended to build 100 Réseau sets, but as the design work was not ready and as both SNCF and GEC Alsthom wanted to maintain the production flow of new trains, the order for Atlantique sets was increased by 10 to 105 and the Réseau build was reduced from 100 to 90. The first Réseau sets entered service in the spring of 1993; the full build of 90 sets was completed by the end of 1995.

Réseau Unit 547 passes Croisilles (KP 149) – the junction for Arras – at 300 km/h en route from Paris Nord to Lille Flandres. The track on the left of the picture is the southbound chord from the Arras classic line which joins TGV Nord Europe towards Paris. *Colin Marsden*

THALYS PBA power car about to be lowered on to its bogies on the GEC Alsthom production line at Belfort. *GEC Alsthom*

Technically the Réseau trains are eight-car versions of the Atlantique trains. They have eight 1,100 kW synchronous traction motors on four motor bogies providing a total output of 8,800 kW; maximum speed is 300 km/h (186 mph). Their external profile is similar to the Atlantique trains. They are fitted with the Scharfenberg coupler for multiple-unit working with another Réseau or a Duplex trainset. There are two important differences. To obviate passenger discomfort passing through tunnels at high speeds, they are pressure-sealed. Because most PSE stations can only accommodate two eight-vehicle trainsets (length 400.38 metres) and as it is not possible to modify the large number of platforms and station layouts at acceptable cost, the number of trailers has been restricted to eight.

Réseau configuration is similar to the PSE sets, but again points of detail are different. There are three first class cars (R1, R2 and R3) with 120 seats, a coach with a bar and 16 second class seats (R4), and four second class coaches R5, R6, R7 and R8. Apart from six semi-compartment seats at the end of each first class coach, the stylish 'Club' quatro and duo seating in the Atlantique sets has not been perpetuated for the Réseau sets; the layout is mostly 'Coach' open plan with a mixture of facing and uni-directional seating. As with the Atlantique sets the space at the end of R1 and R8 – used to house a motor block on the PSE trainsets – has been used for passengers. R1 has 36 seats plus 6 in the *salon*. There is a galley between R1 and R2 for the at-seat service of meals. A space for one handicapped passenger plus wheelchair is located in R1. Mindful of longer journeys, the level of second class accommodation has been raised. Seats are reclinable and the pitch is longer; consequently R5, R6 and R7 have 56 seats compared with 60 in the original PSE trainsets. There is a family area and adjoining nursery toilet in R7; the space at the end of R8 – the kiosk – has 17 places. Telephones are located in R2 and R6. There are 11 first class and 15 second class vestibule tip-up seats. A baggage compartment – with six square metres of space – is located in R1 with a maximum capacity of 1.5 tonnes.

In November 1987 SNCF acquired a special test vehicle designed to work marshalled in a normal TGV rake, if necessary in public service. Designated VEGV *Voiture D'Essais Grande Vitesse* (or high-speed test coach), also known as Mélusine, the coach is 24.13 metres long compared with the normal TGV vehicle of 18.7 metres. It is designed to be marshalled between the power car and adjoining trailers in a TGV set. Partly for aesthetic reasons but also to locate an observation post for viewing pantograph performance, the roof is contoured to match the rest of the set. VEGV is equipped with a wide range of electronic equipment for measuring all aspects of technical performance. It is shown here passing through Montgergn Crosenay in the south east Paris suburbs. *Colin Marsden*

There are four different Réseau types:

Two-voltage (Unit 501 to 550). Fifty trainsets, equipped for 25 kV ac and 1.5 kV dc, painted in standard SNCF blue-grey TGV livery and deployed on French domestic services. Thirty-nine sets are based at Le Landy for services from Paris Nord to Northern France plus inter-regional services from Lille Europe to the South East and West of France. Eleven units are based at Paris Sud Est for services from Paris to Nice and Marseille.

Three-voltage (Version 1) (Units 4507 to 4530). Same as two voltage version above but equipped additionally with 3 kV dc and Belgian cab-signalling for working to Brussels. These trains are used on services from Brussels to Nice and other parts of France.

Three-voltage (Version 2) (Units 4501 to 4506). Equipped with modified pantographs for working into Italy and apparatus for decoding Italian (FS) cab-signalling system. SNCF livery stock based at Paris Sud Est.

Three-voltage (Version 3) (Units 4531 to 4540 PBA). Dedicated units for the Paris, Brussels, Amsterdam services. Equipped with Faiveley CX pantographs and TBL cab-signalling for working over Netherlands tracks to Amsterdam. THALYS external livery and internal décor (see Chapter 21) based at Le Landy.

Réseau and Duplex contrasting profiles at Lyon Perrache station.
Brian Perren

TGV Réseau: motor block.
GEC Alsthom

EUROSTAR – TRANS MANCHE SUPER TRAIN

11

A key element in Eurotunnel's bid to secure the concession to fund, build and operate the Channel Tunnel fixed link was the agreement to hire-out 50% of the tunnel capacity to British and French railways for international passenger and freight traffic. Given that two-thirds of the 307.3-mile distance (around half the journey time) from Waterloo International to Paris Nord is over TGV Nord Europe tracks, it was inevitable that the Trans Manche Super Train – now known as Eurostar – would incorporate many of the basic TGV characteristics.

The challenge was how to adapt the proven TGV design to meet the more restricted British loading gauge, take current supplies from the 750 dc third-rail system, and incorporate the very stringent safety criteria for passage of the Channel Tunnel imposed by the Inter-governmental Safety Commission.

A contract to build an initial fleet of 30 high-speed trains was signed in Brussels on 18 December 1989, by the chairmen of BR, SNCF and SNCB. The original order was subsequently increased to a total of 38. Ownership is 18 Eurostar UK (formerly British Rail European Passenger Services now owned by London & Continental Railways Ltd, which has won the contract to build the Channel Tunnel Rail Link), 16 SNCF and four SNCB.

This London to Paris Eurostar is passing Continental Junction, located next to Dollands Moor freight yard, and is preparing to enter the Channel Tunnel. The changeover from 750 V dc third-rail current collection to 25 kV ac and arming the cab-signalling systems are undertaken at the normal 160 km/h (100 mph) line speed. *Colin Marsden*

Standard class seating in Eurostar is a mixture of face-to-face and unidirectional. *Colin Marsden*

Interior of First Class Eurostar, showing the wider seats. *Capital Transport*

To meet the required safety criteria and to optimise paths through the Channel Tunnel, Eurostar trainsets are formed with two half-sets each comprising a power car and nine trailers. Basic TGV formations are usually eight trailers (10 in the case of the Atlantique fleet) with seats for around 370 passengers; for busy journeys two units are coupled to work in multiple. As it would not have been possible to transfer passengers from one of the two separate units to the other in the event of an emergency, this was not an option for the TMST. Channel Tunnel trains must have a locomotive at each end so that, in the event of a fire or another emergency, the train can be divided and one of the locomotives used to take the train and all of the passengers out of the tunnel.

The designers decided to opt for an arrangement which is the equivalent – both in terms of train length and seats – of two TGVs. This produced a 393.72-metre train in four separate elements – two power cars and two separate nine-car half-sets. Trainset formation is M1, R1 to R18 and M2. Vehicles R1 and R18 through to R9 and R10 are the same, so each half-set is identical. Normally the same two half-sets will remain together, although they will be separated for maintenance. If a half-set is unavailable another half-set can be substituted. There are 31 18-coach sets for the core service between London (Waterloo International), Paris Nord and Brussels Midi.

To provide through trains from Paris and Brussels to points beyond London in the UK regions including Birmingham, Manchester, Newcastle, Edinburgh and Glasgow, Eurostar UK has a small sub-fleet of 318.92-metre 14-coach Regional Eurostar trains. This is the maximum length that can be accommodated at most of these UK stations; apart from some minor differences in some of the coaches and technical items in the power cars, the trains are similar.

This outbound London to Brussels Eurostar is approaching Saltwood Tunnel towards the end of its transit through the South East England third-rail network. At the other end of the tunnel the train will change from 750 dc third-rail to 25 kV ac for Channel Tunnel and TGV Nord Europe. Because of its strategic importance the section of route between Ashford International and the Channel Tunnel is signalled for full bi-directional working – hence the running signals on both tracks. *Brian Perren*

To travel over the British third-rail 750 dc network, Eurostars are fitted with current collection shoes. To conform with the standard European gauge, the shoes are retracted before the trains enter the Channel Tunnel.
Colin Marsden

Three different power supply systems are required for the journey from London to Paris or Brussels. All TGV routes, all of the classic SNCF routes in Northern France, Eurotunnel and the British East and West Coast main lines use 25kV ac power supplies; SNCB has 3kV dc; and 750 dc taken from the third-rail is the norm for all British routes south of the Thames, with the new exception of the two or so miles of new track from Continental Junction (including Dollands Moor exchange siding) and the interface with Eurotunnel. Eurostars are designed to work off all three systems.

As the three railway partners gained experience of the cross channel market, they have begun to consider the possibility of direct services from the UK (London and Ashford) to destinations beyond the original boundaries of Paris and Brussels. The first such extension – launched in 1996 – was a service to Marne-le-Vallée (for Disneyland Paris), located on the Jonction line which has 25 kV power supplies. However, for access to other destinations the trains have to be modified to work with 1.5 kV dc necessary to reach important French destinations such as Dijon, Lyon, the French Alps, Marseille and Bordeaux. Having identified Bourg-St-Maurice as a possible Eurostar market for winter sports, four SNCF-owned sets have been equipped to take 1.5 kV dc power supplies and used for a winter weekend service between Waterloo International and Bourg-St-Maurice in the heart of the French Alps from December 1997.

Eurostars are fitted with two separate pantographs – a Faiveley GPU for 25kV and Brecknell Willis for 3kV – plus collector shoes for the third-rail. Voltage changeover – on the move at full line speed – is made as trains pass through a short neutral section. Here the driver lowers the appropriate pantograph, cruises through the neutral section without power, and then raises the other pantograph when the train is fully under the new section. A similar procedure applies for raising or lowering the third-rail current collector shoes; these have to be raised for running on continental tracks where they would otherwise be out of gauge.

To provide sufficient power to move this 18-coach 752-tonne train at a top speed of 300 km/h, each train has a total of twelve 1,020kW asynchronous traction motors. These provide a continuous rating of 12,200kW in 25kV mode, 5,700kW in 3kV mode and 3,400kW in 750V dc mode; 12,200kW is the equivalent of 16,353 hp – a power-weight ratio of 21.75 hp per tonne. Continuous 1.5 kV rating for the three modified sets is 2,700kW. To keep within the 17-tonne axle-load stipulation for SNCF high-speed lines, power is distributed through six motor bogies in a similar configuration to the PSE trainsets. Each power car has two motor bogies and another motor bogie is located under the outer end of R1 and R18 adjoining the two power cars. The traction system consists of six independent motor blocks – one for each of the six motor bogies. These are responsible for traction and for two motors for each motor bogie, including its auxiliaries. One of the motor blocks is also located in the compartment at the outer end of R1 and R18 over the motor bogie.

A significant feature of Eurostar's traction package is the three-phase drive asynchronous traction motor. Originally only suitable for industrial purposes, the asynchronous commutatorless motor is particularly robust, less expensive to maintain and provides about 50% more power than a conventional dc motor for the equivalent bulk and space.

There are two braking systems: on the trailer bogie, braking uses friction through brake pads applied to four brake discs on each axle. For the motor bogies, the traction motors function as generators in combination with brake pads; the current produced by the traction motors is dissipated through a rheostat. With this system the wheels absorb less energy which extend their life span.

Eurostar's British maintenance base is at North Pole near Wormwood Scrubs in West London. The emergency Scharfenberg coupling can be seen on one of the units. *Colin Marsden*

While it is soon apparent that the Eurostar is part of the TGV family, the front end is quite different from earlier TGV types. The profile has been carefully designed to reduce aerodynamic pressure in the tunnel. To minimise possible driver discomfort caused by the flicker of the Channel Tunnel concrete segments, the view from the cab has a specific focus. Consequently, the driving desk is positioned in the centre of the cab rather than on the left side, hitherto standard for both British and French locomotive types. There is an on-board computer system for identifying and diagnosing problems, either for the on-board facilities such as air-conditioning or with the traction and power equipment. The power and brake controllers are UIC standard – forward to supply power and backward to activate the rheostatic braking. The various power supply systems mentioned earlier are controlled by a selector knob.

There are four different types of cab signalling equipment:

TVM430: TVM430 is installed throughout TGV Nord Europe, the Channel Tunnel and the Belgian high-speed line.

'Crocodile': *KVB* Crocodile (so called because the track magnets between the rails resemble a crocodile), is the standard form of audible cab warning system applicable on the classic routes throughout France; it is now being enhanced with KVB, a system of automatic train protection. This system is necessary so that Eurostars can run from the end of TGV Nord Europe and into the terminus at Paris Nord as well as using diversionary routes should this be necessary.

Transmission Balise Locomotive: TBL is the Belgian system for classic SNCB routes.

Automatic Warning Systems (AWS): This is the system known as AWS applicable throughout the British network.

The Eurostar fleet operates on a common basis, although the trains have a home depot according to ownership:

Eurostar UK 18 trains (including seven Regional sets) based at North Pole on the West London Line.

SNCF 16 trains based at Le Landy, a short distance from Paris Nord.

SNCB Four trains based at Forest, a short distance from Brussels Midi.

There are 770 seats in a basic (Three Capitals) Eurostar, 210 in first class and 560 in standard class. (Originally there were 584 second class places but in the light of operating experience seats have been removed from R1/R18, R2/R17, R3/R16, R4/R15 and R5/R14 to provide space for increased baggage stacks). With the identical configuration of each half set, all of the six first class coaches are in the centre of each rake. As with normal British practice, the two catering service cars are positioned between the first and standard class seating areas. Two catering service cars – R6 and R13 – have no normal seating, being devoted entirely to food and drink service. At the standard class end of this coach there is an attractive and spacious bar and lounge area for use of all passengers; at the opposite end there is a galley for the service of meals to all first class passengers at their seats. R6 galley serves into R7, R8 and R9 while R13 galley serves into R12, R11 and R10.

Standard class seating is 2+2 open plan with a central gangway. Face-to-face seats – groups of four with a table in the centre on either side of the centre gangway – are in the middle of R2/R17, R3/R16, R4/R15 and R5/R14 at the point where the two separate unidirectional groups of seats meet. Because R1 and R18 have the motor block compartment at the outer end of the coach, the internal layout is different and has 40 face-to-face seats with tables; 16 of these are in a separate cabin with slightly more space for families. There is a nursery toilet adjacent to this area. Each coach has one or more baggage stacks and toilets; a telephone located in R4 and R15. Seat pitch is about the same as a long-haul airliner and perfectly acceptable for a three-hour journey at budget prices. Décor is light grey offset by yellow; good lighting precludes any sense of claustrophobia that may be felt during the passage of the tunnel.

First class seating is 2+1 open plan with a central gangway, of which 144 seats are face-to-face; all seats have tables with a small lamp. Coaches R7/R12 and R8/R11 have a small relaxation area at the end; a telephone is located in R8/R11. Décor is themed in grey and maroon.

Each set has two spaces for passengers travelling in wheelchairs located in R9/R10 adjacent to a handicapped persons' toilet. All toilets are retention-type. R9/R10 also has the office for customs and frontier police. The train manager's office is located in R2/R17. There are ample exits and each coach has a steel fire protection door at each end. With compulsory reservation every passenger will have a specific seat, but there are 52 tip-up seats throughout the train. Access to the train is through large power-operated plug doors operated by the train manager. Power-operated moveable steps for boarding either from a 500 mm continental platform or from a traditional 915 mm high British platform. In the tunnel there is a platform for emergency evacuation but as this is further from the track than is normal the train provides for this eventuality.

Rail is an inherently safe form of transport. Nonetheless passage of tunnels as long as 50.5 km (31.4 miles) does extend the parameters of underground operations well beyond what was normal in the past. Consequently, stringent safety features have been incorporated into Channel Tunnel operating procedures. In addition to TVM430 cab signalling – which includes full train protection – requirements set by the Inter-governmental Safety Commission and incorporated into the Eurostar design include: use of materials meeting the strictest fire resistant standards; installation of an automatic system of fire protection and fire fighting in each of the motor compartments in the power cars; fire break doors designed to prevent the spread of the fire from one carriage to the next; and the ability to divide the trainset.

DUPLEX

Estimates show that traffic on the PSE line is growing to the extent that there will be insufficient capacity to cope with the business on offer at certain peak times. A similar situation on TGV Nord Europe between Paris and Lille could also arise in the longer-term. Not only has travel between Paris and points in South East France exceeded the original estimates, but new traffic has also been generated as extensions to the original route have been commissioned. While growth can be contained for the next few years, the opening of TGV Méditerranée about 2000 will pose a major challenge. With a journey time of just 3 hours between Paris and Marseille/Montpellier – a reduction of around 1 hour 10 minutes – SNCF expects to gain a significant share of the existing air market plus new traffic generated because the journey time over the 708 km (485 miles) (average speed 260 km/h: 161 mph) between Paris and Marseille is so competitive. SNCF is developing a number of inter-related projects to increase the capacity and speed of the PSE line including double-deck trainsets – the TGV Duplex.

Below: Duplex Unit 201 after an evening arrival at Paris Gare de Lyon. *Brian Perren*

Right: Duplex power car profile. *Brian Perren*

While resignalling the PSE could provide an extra three train paths per hour, the problem of concentrated peak-period demand remains. Increasing the number of seats per train was the next option, normally achieved by extending the length of the train. Although some two-unit Atlantique services run from the west of France to Lyon offering a total of 970 seats, there are only a few Sud Est stations which can accommodate two Atlantique sets in multiple, the total length of which is 475.18 metres. This is 75 metres longer than two PSE or Réseau sets. Extending platforms to accommodate longer TGV trainsets was neither a practical or financially-viable option.

Given successful development of double-deck trainsets for busy commuter routes, with similar pressing line capacity problems, in 1987, SNCF – in association with GEC Alsthom – launched a feasibility study to determine if the double-deck concept could be successfully married with the proven TGV technology. Hitherto, all TGV and derivative trainsets – PSE, Atlantique, Eurostar and Réseau – have been designed with low-slung bodies, articulated bogies and within a 17-tonne axle-load. At an early stage the designers considered using standard non-articulated trailers, but while this would have simplified the challenge of meeting the 17-tonne axle-load, this was the only tangible benefit. It became clear that by using aluminium for the bodyshells the basic TGV design criteria could be retained. With the technical feasibility of the train now confirmed, work to assess its commercial viability could now begin. Full-scale static models of coach layouts were build at Le Landy Depot, followed by the conversion of two PSE trailers (one first and one second class) to simulate the lower and upper-deck of the Duplex cars for testing in public passenger service. Feedback from passenger research was sufficiently positive for SNCF to give the go-ahead for the project. In June 1991 SNCF placed an order with GEC Alsthom for 85 trains, 30 firm and 55 on option.

In October 1991 trials were started with a test rake using three prototype vehicles – an end vehicle and two intermediate trailers – hauled by two Atlantique power cars. These were used for both static and running tests to evaluate a range of factors such as passenger comfort, vibration levels, acoustic levels and the efficiency of the air-conditioning system.

Of all the design challenges, meeting the 17-tonne static axle-load was the most difficult to achieve. Long extruded aluminium profiles for the bodyshells were formed from alloys with a balance between mechanical strength, weldability and corrosion resistance. A combination of factors including the use of hollow axles, changes to the brake discs, the use of aluminium instead of steel for air reservoirs and other equipment, enabled the weight of a fully-equipped bogie to be reduced by more than one tonne. A new seat design – weighing only 14 kg compared with 20 kg for an Atlantique seat – contributed to the savings. Thin insulated cable allowed 200 kg to be saved on each coach.

While the Duplex was conceived as a high-capacity train, the opportunity has been taken to provide more passenger space and comfort, including improved air-conditioning capable of supplying two decks and improved sound insulation down to a noise level of only 68 dB(A) on the lower deck at the full 300 km/h speed. The train is pressure-sealed. There is more room, particularly in second class where the space between unidirectional seats has been extended to 920 mm; space between face-to-face seats is 1,900 mm. All seats – in both first and second class – align with windows. Other features include: reclinable seats in second as well as first class; ergonomically designed headrests; moveable armrests; foot rests and individual reading lights.

Facing page upper: Although the motivation for the Duplex train was to provide more seats within the standard TGV eight-car formation, the opportunity has been taken to provide more passenger space and comfort. Access is through a central gangway along the upper deck as shown in this illustration of the second class accommodation. *Brian Perren*

Facing page lower: More leg room and space is the feature of the lower-deck first class section which offers quiet ambience for passengers to work or relax. *Brian Perren*

A Duplex consists of two power cars and eight trailers. Access to the train is through a single wide door positioned at the end of each coach, leading to a spacious vestibule and the stairway to the upper deck. Passage through the train is along the upper-deck and across the vehicle articulation over the bogies. The seven lower deck saloons are self-contained. To reach the buffet, lower deck passengers must use the stairway to the upper-deck to pass through the train. Seat reservations will be sold offering a choice of 'panoramic' upper deck seats or 'quiet' seats for those who prefer the privacy of the lower deck. Only the upper part of the catering service car (R4) has been used for passenger accommodation; the lower part is used to house all of the train's auxiliary equipment. To give more headroom, the floor of the bar area is slightly lower than the other upper-deck saloons. As well as the spacious bar area, R4 also has a small aircraft-style galley for the at-seat meal service to first class passengers in the upper-decks of R2 and R3. There is also a small office for the train *contrôler*.

Seating in both classes is a mixture of unidirectional and face-to-face. Seating for families – also a feature in Atlantique, Réseau and Eurostar sets – is provided in the upper level of R6. There is a one space for a handicapped passenger with wheelchair in the lower-deck of R1; here there is a small platform to lower the wheelchair down to the lower-deck level.

The styling of the power cars – which have a more rounded appearance than first and second generation TGV builds – has been chosen to improve aerodynamic performance and define the train's image as a third-generation TGV. Technical performance is similar to the Réseau sets. Each power car has four 1,100 kW synchronous traction motors, 4,400 kW per power car, giving a total output of 8,800 kW (11,796 hp) for the complete train. Power to weight ratio is 31 hp/tonne; this compares with 22.35/tonne for the first PSE series, 24.37 for the Atlantique series, 21.74 for Eurostar and 30.79 for the latest Réseau series. Power supply is 25 kV ac and 1.5 kV dc; SNCF is studying the possibility of adding 3 kV dc to the train so that they can work through to Brussels. A fourth voltage – 15 kV 16 2/3 Hz – giving access to Germany and Switzerland is also a long-term possibility. Scharfenberg automatic couplers are fitted for multiple working with another Duplex or with a Réseau set. Driving cab layout is based on the latest ergonomic research. To give improved vision particularly for left or right-hand driving, the driving position has been moved to the centre of the cab.

TGV Duplex is a remarkable train. As well as building a train with 516 seats – 45% more than a Réseau set – but within the same weight and length dimensions as earlier two-plus-eight trainsets, the designers have been able to incorporate a significant number of passenger improvements. The rate of return for a Duplex is 15% better than a single-deck TGV. The staircase to the upper-deck is reminiscent of a Boeing 747. Décor is attractive. Legroom is generous. But the upper-deck toilet is not very large.

One trainset was delivered in spring 1995 for technical and passenger evaluation trials. Series deliveries started in July 1995 and commercial services on the Paris-Lyon route began in December 1996. Total cost of the 30 trainsets is FFR 3.5 billion – approximately £466 million, say £15.5 million per train. If Channel Tunnel safety criteria could be met, the Duplex could be used on services from Europe to St Pancras via the new Rail Link.

Supplies are loaded into the upper deck of the Catering Service car (R4) by forklift truck. *Alan Williams*

Left: A complete coach – R4 – has been used to provide a spacious bar and lounge area on the Duplex upper-deck. *Colin Marsden*

Below left: To provide better vision and space for the increasing number of in-cab signalling systems, the Duplex driving position has been moved to the centre of the cab. This central position has also been adapted for Eurostar and PBKA. *Colin Marsden*

Below: Each coach has a spacious stairway to the upper deck. *Colin Marsden*

Starting with the original PSE series in 1976, the French train builder De Dietrich has participated in all TGV construction up to and including the first tranche of trains for Korea. The picture shows the end Duplex vehicle with a full bogie at one end and a shared bogie for the articulation at the other end. *De Dietrich*

TGV DUPLEX TRAIN FORMATION				
	DETAILS	SEATING		
			FIRST	SECOND
M1	Power Car			
R1	First Class: non-smoking 38 upper, 26 lower deck; 5.5sq metre baggage compartment; space for handicapped passenger and wheelchair; special toilet. Standard toilet.		64	
R2	First Class: non-smoking 32 upper, 28 lower deck. Two toilets. Telephone.		60	
R3	First Class: 32 upper deck non-smoking, 28 lower deck smoking. Two toilets.		60	
R4	Catering service car. Upper deck bar and galley for at-seat meal service; conductor's office. Lower deck used for train auxiliary equipment.			
R5	Second Class: smoking 42 upper deck non-smoking, 38 lower deck smoking. Two toilets.			80
R6	Second Class: non-smoking 42 upper 38 lower deck. Family seating. Two toilets.			80
R7	Second Class: non-smoking 42 upper, 38 lower deck. Family seating. Nursery. Two toilets.			80
R8	Second Class: non-smoking 54 upper, 38 lower deck. Baggage compartment. Two toilets. Telephone.			92
M2	Power car			
	SEATING TOTALS		184	332
	GRAND TOTAL		516	
M - Motrice (Power car) R - Remorque (Trailer)				

PARIS–BRUSSELS–COLOGNE–AMSTERDAM

A major task as the European high-speed network gains momentum is designing trains which can cope with the different national power supply and cab-signalling systems. While these long-standing technical differences are a fact of life, there is a considerable scope for technical harmonisation so that the operating range of new-generation international trainsets can be maximised. The UIC, the national railways and the railway industry have formed a working group – *L'Association Européenne Pour L'Interopérabilité Ferroviaire* – to produce standard technical specifications for the interoperability of trainsets between neighbouring countries.

So far, basic TGVs – plus the Eurostar derivative – have been designed with up to three traction current supply systems, enabling operation of through services from France into Switzerland, Britain, Belgium and Italy. When the THALYS service was expanded in December 1997 to serve Köln (Cologne) as well as Amsterdam, a total of four different current supply systems were required – 25 kV from Paris to the approaches to Brussels and over the upgraded or new lines beyond Brussels to the German frontier, 3 kV in Belgium, 1.5 kV from the Belgian border into the Netherlands and 15 kV 16 2/3 Hz in Germany.

Four-voltage power units are not new. The first such train for cross-border working was the Swiss RABe EuroCity multiple units built in 1961 for the Trans European Express network. Electrical equipment was packed in a six-axle 100-tonne power car in the centre of the unit. Three years later, Alsthom built a six-axle four-voltage, 109-tonne locomotive (CC40101 series) for SNCF through workings between Paris and Brussels/Liège; an identical version of this locomotive (Class 18) was built for SNCB.

PBKA and three-voltage coupled Réseau power cars stand side-by-side at Le Landy. *Regis Chessum*

Although it looks quite different, the 17-unit THALYS PBKA series has a basic eight-car Réseau formation, but with a power car based on the aluminium-bodied Duplex. Passenger accommodation and internal décor is identical to the PBA Réseau series, but the power car with its four-voltage systems and five cab-signalling systems is much more complex. Pre-series Unit 4341 at Paris Nord in June 1996. *Colin Marsden*

Pre-series Unit 4341 under test on the German high-speed line between Fulda and Würzburg. *Christoph Assie*

In accordance with European competition rules, the four railways – SNCF, SNCB, NS and DB AG – issued a tender for a four-voltage high-speed train for the Paris, Brussels, Köln (Cologne), Amsterdam (PBKA) corridor. GEC Alsthom and Siemens – the builders of the successful Inter City Express high-speed train for the German railways – were the preferred bidders.

Some considerable time elapsed between the invitation to tender and the response by GEC Alsthom and Siemens. GEC Alsthom's bid was about 20% higher than the price level envisaged by the four railways while Siemens' was even higher. Discussions continued between the railways and the bidders to see if the price could be reduced to an acceptable level. Rather than go back to the drawing board for a fresh start, the builders were asked to reduce the level of interior fittings in the train. Given these new parameters, GEC Alsthom produced a new version of its train – basically a four-voltage TGV Réseau – a derivative of the three-voltage train described earlier. Even so, the modified Réseau design was still about 15% more than the railways had originally hoped to pay.

The PBKA has a Réseau configuration, but with a redesigned power car. Given the need not only to provide space for five different cab-signalling systems, but also to give better vision for left or right-hand running, it was necessary to move the driving position from the side to the centre of the cab as is the case with the Eurostar and Duplex trains. In all essential respects the PBKA power car is a four-voltage version of the imposing two-voltage Duplex power car.

The trains are powered by eight 1,100 kW synchronous traction motors producing 8,800 kW in ac mode, 4,460 kW in 15 kV 16 2/3 Hz mode, 3,680 kW in 1.5 and 3 kV dc mode. Other technical details are the same as the Réseau fleet. Externally and internally the trains have been painted and decorated to carry the THALYS brand name. Series numbering is 4341 to 4358. Originally 27 trainsets were ordered, but as the Brussels-German Frontier section of TGV Belge will not now open until around 2005 the order has been temporarily cut back to 17 trains. Ownership is: nine SNCB, six SNCF and two NS; two of the SNCB trainsets will be leased to DBAG. Trainsets will be based at Le Landy (Paris) and Forest (Brussels).

Amsterdam Central – Paris Nord THALYS service arriving in Rotterdam Central. *Brian Perren*

TRAIN SUPERVISION AND CAB SIGNALLING

Given the different characteristics of the Paris Sud Est line – long sections of route with few junctions or intermediate stations, dedicated trainsets, and very much higher train speeds than those on classic lines – SNCF introduced an entirely new system of traffic regulation and signalling. Train supervision, operation of points, control of power supplies, and day-to-day operational disposal of trainsets were brought together in a new centralised control centre known as *Poste d'Aiguillage et de Regulation* (PAR). Using the central PAR display panel which shows the position of every train on the route, the operators initiate crossover and junction movements through small switches which activate the equipment at the remote satellite signalling installation. On the Paris Sud Est line and the Atlantique line these are known as *Poste tout Relais à transit Souple* (PRS), or selection by one switch. On the Nord Europe, Jonction and Rhône Alpes lines a more advanced computer-based control – *Poste tout Relais à Commande Informatisée* (PRCI) – is used. All TGV remote control posts are denoted by lineside markerboards – eg PRS 25 at Mâcon Loché station – which are also used as timing reference points in working timetables and driver's schedule documentation. PRS and PRCI marker boards are visible from the train windows.

The second Paris Sud Est line innovation was in-cab signalling with full Automatic Train Protection (ATP). Signalling is the means of communication between operating personnel on the ground and train drivers, the basic purpose of which is the organisation of train movements in a safe and efficient manner. There are three main functions – correct routeing of trains to avoid conflict with other train movements at stations and other places where tracks merge; the spacing out of trains travelling in the same direction on the same track so that they can stop within a safe distance behind the preceding train; and the prevention of trains travelling in the opposite direction on the same track, although this is a problem normally associated with single-track routes or routes signalled for two-way (bidirectional) working.

It is a tribute to those engineers who pioneered the development of railway signalling that rail continues to be the safest of all transport modes. Hitherto classic railway signalling has been based on the simple concept of trackside signals which tell the driver the state of the line ahead to ensure safe operation. Practice varies from country to country, but three aspects are in common use: red for stop, green for safe to proceed, and yellow to warn that the next signal is red giving advance warning to slow down and stop. While these basic principles – supported by audible warning systems in driving cabs – are perfectly satisfactory for speeds up to 200–220 km/h on classic routes, a more advanced system is required for trains running at TGV speeds. Visual reaction to lineside signals is no longer a practical possibility at 270 km/h, 300 km/h or even 350 km/h. To cope with these new levels of speed, CSEE Transport and SNCF developed a new system of cab-signalling – TVM 300 – for the Paris-Sud Est line. TVM is a French acronym for *Transmission Voie Machine*, i.e. track-to-train transmission. TVM 300 works as follows. As with all signalling systems – cab or lineside – the first factor to be determined is the distance required for the train to come from its maximum permitted speed to a complete stop. Using full emergency braking, a TGV travelling at 270 km/h needs 3 km (1.9 miles) of level track to stop. In day-to-day service conditions less severe braking is needed and it may only be necessary for the train to reduce its speed and not come to a complete stop. Theoretical stopping distances are 6,300 metres (4 miles) from 270 km/h on the Sud Est and 8,000 metres from 300 km/h on the Atlantique line.

To facilitate the braking of the train, but also to reduce the headway between successive trains and consequently increase the capacity of the route, these theoretical stopping distances have been divided into three or four parts each constituting a 'block section' in signalling terms. Progress from block to block is detected by track circuits which monitor the state of the line ahead. The state of these track circuits is picked up from the rails by a receiver on the underside of the power car and decoded through an on-board microprocessor. This data is then used to advise the driver the target speed at which he must enter the next block section. Block sections – or section reference – are indicated by trackside markerboards (*repères*) positioned at driver's eye level throughout TGV routes. These are square-shaped with a yellow triangle on a blue background with a point towards the track to which the *repère* applies. As most TGV lines are signalled for full bi-directional running, most *repères* are positioned in pairs on either side of the line with the point towards the appropriate track. The target speed is shown on a digital display on the driver's console. The displays are:

- maximum speed allowed at the next *repère* VL (vitesse limite) – or the maximum speed of the type of train – or 300 km/h displayed by black characters on a green background,

- an indication to reduce speed before the next reference point, either because the line ahead is occupied by another train or the train is approaching a junction or diversion location with a lower speed limit; displayed by black characters on a white background,

- an indication – 000 – ordering the driver to stop at the next reference; displayed by black characters on a red background.

Although TVM 300 is based on absolute safety, it is still considered desirable for the driver to retain manual control of the train at all times, but Automatic Train Protection (ATP) is also an essential part of the equipment. When restrictive information is picked-up, advising the driver that he may have to reduce speed at the next *repère*, an audible warning by horn is given. Thus the driver can control the train with due regard to the characteristics of the line (curvature, gradients etc), effective braking and energy-conservation. If for any reason – possibly because he is incapacitated – the driver fails to respond, ATP will bring the train to a complete stop.

Given the desirability of retaining manual driving control, it is still necessary to give drivers the maximum possible warning of the state of the line ahead. With classic lineside signalling this is provided by a 'distant' or equivalent signal (double or single yellow display in Britain), but this is not practical on TGV. Instead, an additional item – the attention indicator – has been incorporated into the TVM signalling sequence. On the PSE sets the digital display sequence is 270; should it be necessary to warn the driver that he may have to slow down or stop 270 is replaced by 220, 220 by 160, and 160 by 000 (stop). On the Atlantique line 300 is the line speed display, but – and this is the important difference – the next restrictive warning is 300 flashing, followed by 270, 220, 160, 000 (stop).

Data from the rails is present throughout each signal section. A more restrictive item of information (for example 220 replaced by 160 km/h) is only activated at the next *repère* while a non-restrictive item of information (160 replaced by 220 km/h) can be activated before the next *repère*. Such a situation can arise where the train ahead is accelerating away from a speed check and the gap between the two trains has widened. As in classic signalling, the spacing of the block sections depends on the profile of the line at given locations. On all TGV lines there are some shorter sections on rising gradients; these are necessary to maintain the even flow of traffic.

When the Paris Sud Est line was planned the performance specification was a 2-hour journey time between Paris and Lyon Part-Dieu, with a five-minute headway and a maximum speed of 270 km/h, even though the line is designed – but not yet signalled – for a potential maximum speed of 300 km/h. In the late 1970s these parameters were well ahead of anything previously set for conventional railways in Europe. Following the commercial success of the Paris Sud Est line, which generated significant levels of new rail travel and paved the way for other new lines to be built, the position has now been reached where capacity must be increased to cope with the volume of business on offer. To remain competitive, speeds must also increase so that journey times can be further reduced. It is for this reason that TGV Nord Europe has been equipped with the more sophisticated TVM 430 allowing a 3-minute headway between trains running at a maximum speed between 300 and 330 km/h.

When TVM 300 was installed on the PSE line it was state of the art. Following research the system has now been developed to a point where 27 continuous pieces of information can be transmitted from the track to the train as opposed to only 18 in TVM 300. This is why TVM 430 has been installed on TGV Nord Europe and the southern section of TGV Rhône Alpes. It has also been chosen by Eurotunnel for the Channel Tunnel; here block sections will be shorter and the maximum speed 160 km/h.

Given the ability to transmit and decode a much greater number of data items, it was possible to extend the system to include indications of distance and profile as well as continuous advice regarding the state of the line ahead. This has made it possible to construct a control curve adjusted to the speed and profile of each block section. Whereas TVM 300 can only accommodate one 'attention indicator' aspect – that is 270 flashing on the Sud Est and the 300 flashing on the Atlantique line – TVM 430 can produce a continuous flow of information in a situation where the line ahead is occupied by the preceding train.

Thus, if the line ahead is blocked, the TVM 430 digital display will show flashing 300, flashing 270, flashing 230, flashing 170, as it passes through the block sections followed by 000 if the train has to stop. As drivers will be receiving earlier advice of restrictive information rather than having to wait for the display to change at the next *repère* they can anticipate their brake application and deceleration by some vital seconds. Thus, the length of block sections can be reduced without prejudicing safety. ATP automatic override is set at 10 or 20 km/h above the theoretical manual deceleration curve; the margin is higher at the end of a section showing 000.

By a continuous display of 'attention indicators' and the consequent impact on braking distances, it is now possible to reduce the length of a block section from 2,000 metres (1.2 miles) to 1,500 metres (0.9 miles), shortening up by 500 metres (0.3 miles). On the face of things this is a small reduction, but when applied throughout a route such as TGV Nord Europe it gives a headway of three minutes with a maximum speed of 300 km/h.

How TVM cab-signalling has been enhanced can be more readily appreciated from the table. On the Paris Sud Est line (see diagram below) with TVM 300 and block sections of 2,100 metres (1.3 miles), the space between two trains is 13,000 metres (8.0 miles) or 2 minutes 54 seconds running time. With 270 flashing showing on the driver's console, the slow-down sequence is 220, 160 and 000 bringing the train to a complete standstill two block sections (ie 4,400 metres or 2.7 miles) to the rear of the train ahead.

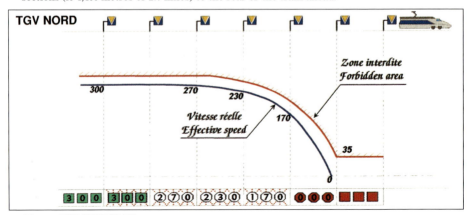

On the Atlantique line TVM 300 has been installed to cope with 300 km/h and block sections of 2,100 metres (1.3 miles). Because Atlantique trains are longer, the spacing between trains has been extended to 14,480 metres (9.0 miles) but running time remains 2 minutes 54 seconds. The sequence shown on the driver's console is: steady 300 for normal running followed by a flashing attention indicator 300, then steady displays of 270, 220, 160 and 000.

Turning now to TGV Nord Europe the benefits of TVM 430 are readily apparent. With a continuous display of flashing attention indications this is the stopping sequence: flashing 300, flashing 270, flashing 230, flashing 170 followed by 000. Consequently, the spacing between the two trains – trains on this line are shorter – is reduced to 10,900 metres (6.8 miles), or 2 minutes 11 seconds running time at 300 km/h on level track.

TVM 430 has also been installed between Grenay and St-Marcel-les-Valence on the southern section of the Rhône Alpes line. As the gradients are relatively severe and as the latest Réseau, Duplex and modified PSE sets have superior braking, TVM 430 will improve traffic flow over this section. Even though TVM 300 is used on the Rhône Alpes northern section (Montanay to Grenay) the line speed is 300 km/h throughout, although unmodified PSE sets can only run at 270 km/h.

Whilst the TVM 430 equipment functions on tracks equipped for TVM 300, the reverse does not apply – TVM 300 on-board equipment does not function with TVM 430 track equipment. Thus all TGV types can run over the Sud Est line as far south as Grenay. To enable PSE sets to work south of Grenay on the Rhône Alpes line to destinations such as Avignon, Montpellier, Marseille and Nice – around 60 of these sets have now been equipped with TVM 430. Similarly, 20 Atlantique sets have been equipped with TVM 430 to cover services from the West and South West of France to Lille. In the next few years, SNCF will probably equip its remaining PSE trainsets with TVM 430 as part of its upgrading plans for this route. Systemwide deployment of all TGV trainsets will then be possible.

Meanwhile, to reduce headway on the PSE line from 5 to 4 minutes, a modification has been made to the TVM 300 equipment on the PSE sets. As described earlier, the original 'line clear' display on the PSE console consisted of two letters VL (*Vitesse Limite*) or normal speed for that part of the route; if the line ahead was not clear VL is replaced by 270 and so on. Now the VL indication has been replaced by 270 – the attention indicator is 270 flashing. Because TVM 300 data is restricted to only 21 pieces of continuous information, the audible warning horn in the cab now functions as the 'attention indicator' for the subsequent speed reduction steps and operates 15 seconds before the approach to the next *repère*. With earlier indication of restrictive information, a driver can brake at the optimum time in relation to the braking distance required. With reduced braking distances, the overlap between two succeeding trains can be reduced to the extent that one block section overlap can be eliminated without prejudicing safety. Over the length of the PSE line this can be used to reduce the existing headway from five to four minutes.

The revised 'attention indicator' procedure will also enable the trains to be signalled over the PSE line at a revised maximum speed of 300 km/h, but this increase is also dependent on other factors including modification of block sections, particularly on rising gradients, and the strengthening of power supplies.

As well as special signalling for high-speed lines, TGVs are also equipped with SNCF's standard in-cab devices for operating domestic services on classic lines in France. These include an audible warning system – *crocodile* – so-called because the track magnet resembles a crocodile, plus the new KVB automatic train protection system. There is another system – the *préanonce* – a device which gives the driver advance warning of the state of the line ahead and which, in conjunction with double-block signalling, enables TGVs to run at 200–220 km/h on certain sections of classic line.

With TGVs – or TGV derivatives – working beyond France into neighbouring countries, additional cab-signalling equipment is now necessary. Because of the wide variety of equipment chosen by other railways, some trainsets such as the THALYS PBKA four-voltage units now require five different cab-signalling systems.

SELLING THE PRODUCT

In earlier chapters we discussed how TGV speeds had been raised to 300 km/h and later in Chapter 29 how the world maximum 515 km/h speed was achieved. These achievements have tangible publicity value, but potential customers are much more concerned with how this technology is transformed into an acceptable product. For it is journey-time – not speed *per se* – that will attract customers. Even so this is not enough. In today's mass travel market – TGV is a train for everybody and not a Concorde of the rails – many other factors contribute to total product quality. Whereas the ambience of the first-generation PSE trainsets was somewhat sparse, on-board facilities now include family seating areas, nursery toilets, enhanced facilities for handicapped travellers, a kiosk for young persons and a conference room for business travellers in first class. TGV has become more user-friendly. Despite the setback caused by the rather hasty launch of the Socrate reservation system, the TGV image has been greatly improved. Welcome booths (*Accueil*) to help passengers with problems are located at all principal Grandes Lignes stations. In the same way as TGV technology has evolved since it was launched in 1981, the way the 'TGV product' is offered to the public has also changed in response to the market and in particular the effect of intensified competition from other modes.

TGV has made a major impact on the French travel scene, but so has the expanding autoroute network. Deregulated airline services are also a serious competitor in the business market, particularly where journeys are around the three-hour threshold where air is equal to rail. Given the need to fight its corner in an increasingly competitive market, SNCF has now moved to a market-led rather than an engineering-led organisation – for technical advances can be funded only from the market place. Recognising the philosophy of customer primacy, SNCF has two key posts at board level. The Directeur General Délégué Clientèles has strategic responsibility for the two main passenger sectors – Grandes Lignes and Ile De France (the greater Paris area) – although day-to-day management of regional services is largely delegated to regional directors. The Directeur General Délégué Exploitation – the other key post – has strategic responsibility for operations, safety, infrastructure etc. The responsibility for the Grandes Lignes business sector is positioned in the Directeur General Délégué Clientèles's domain which also includes responsibility for traction and rolling stock, the provision of which is funded either by the Directeur Grandes Lignes or Directeur Ile De France.

Grandes Lignes products – classic trains as well as TGVs – are based on market segmentation with revenue-generation by yield management. Thus customers on-board a TGV have a range of amenities such as those just mentioned and the price of their tickets will depend on the time, day and flexibility of their travel arrangements. There are two main market segments – business and leisure. Although the majority of business travellers tend to use first class some travel in second class and there is a significant volume of leisure travellers such as senior citizens who choose travel in first class.

Before TGV SNCF's fares were based on the distance travelled with rates for second and first class, although supplements were charged for quality trains such as Trans Europe Express (TEE) services where superior accommodation and good journey-times were on offer. This had to be changed for TGV, which was conceived as a new product for the mass market, the economics of which would be based on revenue generation from an increase in both the size and share of the travel market.

As part of its customer care initiatives SNCF deploys many additional staff to assist passengers on peak days at Paris and its other principal stations throughout the network. This young lady is wearing the distinctive red jacket for Grandes Lignes Grands Departs. As well as identifying its place in the SNCF management structure, the term Grandes Lignes is also used as a national brand name for all long-distance services, approximately 50% of which are now provided by TGV.
Brian Perren

The Business Market

The nature of their needs is such that the business traveller is a very demanding customer. Journeys to business meetings are often arranged at short notice, most wish to arrive at destinations between 0900 and 1000 and, as it is often impossible to predict the length of meetings, they are uncertain regarding their return journeys. To reflect this demand the timetable provides additional trains in the early morning peak – there are six services from Paris all arriving in Lyon by 1000 – and additional services in mid-afternoon. Generally speaking the afternoon peak is more evenly spread. Even though these trains may not be filled on each and every day, this level of service is necessary to retain market share, but the market has to bear the cost of these unpredictable levels of demand. This is why peak fares on business routes such as Paris-Lyon, Paris-Lille, Paris-Nantes and Paris-Bordeaux have a higher price than the same journey on a mid-week or weekend train. But the business traveller has to be offered more than a convenient train, albeit with a larger seat – ability to change his reservation at very short notice, space to park the car and a waiting area similar to those offered for Business Class travellers at airports are all facilities which are now provided by Grandes Lignes.

The Leisure Market

Entirely different factors influence the leisure market. To cover their costs TGV trainsets have to be in service for the maximum number of hours per day. On a busy route such as Paris-Lyon, Paris-Lille, Paris-Brussels (THALYS) or Paris-London (Eurostar) – where the service is hourly for most of the day – the peak business trains will sell very well, but there will invariably be seats to spare during the middle of the day particularly during the winter. These can be filled by a range of discounted fares tailored to the needs of specific market groups, although the viability depends on a firm sale which cannot be changed and certain time-restrictions such as the Saturday-night away, common in airline pricing, are necessary, to avoid abstraction from higher non-discounted fares. Customers buying full-fare tickets pay for the ability to alter their travel arrangements up to the point of departure; lower-fare customers trade-off the discount for a loss of personal flexibility. Grandes Lignes has devised a wide range of 'products' aimed at specific target groups such as children and young people, senior citizens, and couples travelling together.

CROSS FRONTIER SERVICES

To cope with the changing characteristics of international cross-frontier train services – particularly where TGVs have replaced classic locomotive-hauled trains – new arrangements for the management of these services have been set up by SNCF with neighbouring railways. Previously, when traffic levels were comparatively modest, UIC kilometre-trading was an appropriate means of balancing the cost of rolling stock which continued beyond national frontiers to destinations in other countries. Paris-Brussels was a particular case in point. Where an SNCF four-voltage locomotive was used for a journey from Paris to Brussels, SNCB could balance the kilometres incurred by SNCF over their rails with a compensating journey by one of their locomotives to Paris. Because of the cost – and in particular the technical characteristics of TGV trainsets – neighbouring railways including SNCB and NS are now buying THALYS TGV international trainsets to cover their rolling-stock contribution to international services. The Swiss have purchased a PSE trainset from the SNCF to cover its contribution to the France-Swiss route. The only way to optimise the deployment of these international trainsets is by joint management. On these international routes old-style distance-based pricing is now being replaced by route-specific market pricing.

SNCF and its partner administrations recognised that a unified business strategy for each international route could no longer be effectively developed and implemented through the separate organisational hierarchies of two or more railways. The best way forward for routes such as Paris-Lausanne/Berne or Paris-Brussels was to establish single management entities to develop train service proposals, pricing strategy, yield-management and distribution systems, on-board service issues, new liveries and other marketing matters. Each business unit – the establishment of which is by bilateral agreements between the railways – is responsible to the participating railways, but day-to-day operations are implemented locally. SNCF is involved in six such international joint-ventures. They are:

- Groupement d'Intérêt Economique (GIE): Franco Suisse: This first such unit, established in December 1993, is responsible for the Paris-Lausanne/Berne TGV service; good progress has been achieved, including more proactive marketing, TGV services to Brig and Zürich and a new branding, 'La Ligne De Coeur'.

- Westrail International: Established in May 1995 to manage the THALYS (Paris, Brussels, Amsterdam) TGV service.

- Groupement Européen d'Intérêt Economique (GEIE): France-Italy: There are two units – one for overnight and one for daytime services – for France-Italy business. The daytime unit is based in Milan and headed by an Italian Railways manager. The Milan unit manages the Paris-Milan TGV and Milan-Lyon ETR 460 service.

- Eurostar: At present there is no specific joint-venture to manage Eurostar. SNCF's participation in Eurostar is managed by a small management group, Mission Eurostar, based in Paris which co-ordinates all SNCF's activities for this service. As the service is marketed and operated as a single international service, there is close co-operation between SNCF, SNCB and Eurostar UK.

INFORMATION, TIMETABLES, SALES, ON-BOARD FACILITIES

Given the need for a wide range of products and diversity of ticket prices, it is essential that these are widely publicised, easily understood, and that all of the information is readily available. The most suitable booklet for the frequent traveller using a specific route is the A5-size free *Guide du Voyageur* issued for all major trunk routes – TGV and classic services – and is distributed free. Everything the passenger needs to know – including fares – is included. General information is also given in English and German.

There are several ways of buying a ticket for a TGV journey. Most are sold through SNCF stations, all of which are connected to the Socrate computer systems or through appointed travel agents who have the same facilities. The sales clerk consults the Résarail system to check what seats are on offer for the journey required and at what price. The computer will then print and issue the ticket and the whole transaction is completed. Payment by major credit cards is accepted. You can book at any station for any journey. For example, if you are in a small town such as Epernay, you can book seats from Antibes to Paris by TGV without any problem. You can also book and pay for your meal in the first class at-seat meal-service area if you wish. As all seats on TGVs are allocated by computer, seats do not carry reservation tags although every seat is reserved. You locate your seat by reference to your Résa ticket, a seating plan at the end of the coach and the individual seat number.

Two facilities merit special mention. Automatic ticket dispensing machines and 'Minitel'. The automatic dispensers – which are located at selected busy principal stations – work as follows. By pushing the appropriate buttons, you select your destination, day and time of travel, class of travel, seating requirements etc. To complete the transaction you place your credit card into the machine, punch in your PIN and the transaction is completed and the tickets are issued. Booking by Minitel – which is a French version of the British Ceefax system – is basically similar to the automatic dispensers on the stations, except that you make the transaction in your home or office. When the transaction is completed you are given a reference number which enables you to collect your tickets at the station prior to departure. You can also make a reservation by telephone which you collect and pay for at the station prior to departure.

Earlier chapters have described the composition and seating configuration for various TGV types. For passenger information and seat reservation purposes, trainsets are numbered from 1 upwards starting with the first vehicle from the platform buffer-stop end at Paris. Trains starting from the provinces are numbered in reverse order. Coach reservation numbers are the same as the formation numbers – that is R1 to R8 in PSE, Réseau and Duplex sets are coaches 1 to 8 for public purposes and R1 to R10 in Atlantique sets are coaches 1 to 10. When a train consists of two units the rear unit leaving Paris remains the same and the leading unit vehicles are numbered from 11 to 18 in the case of PSE sets or 11 to 20 for Atlantique sets; reverse order applies for trains starting from the provinces bound for Paris. All special facilities – accommodation for handicapped customers, *espace enfants*, the kiosk, and first class *salon* – are included in the reservation network.

TGV CATERING

As the Sud Est project evolved, it was apparent to SNCF that a completely new approach to on-train catering would be necessary to meet the totally changed travel conditions created by TGV. With journey times on main routes cut from four to two hours, significantly increased passenger numbers, higher-density seating, insufficient space to install a fully-equipped train kitchen, plus the intensive use of trainsets, an airline-style modular operation was the only feasible option. For some journeys – Paris-Lille or Paris-Tours for example – where journeys are one hour or even less, an at-seat trolley service may be all that is necessary to meet passengers' needs on these routes.

TGV catering comprises an at-seat service of continental breakfast, lunch or dinner to first class customers plus a take-away bar for all other customers. All food drink and equipment for TGV catering is prepared at shore bases (*Centres d'Avitaillement*), loaded into mobile modules and taken by tractor to be loaded onto the train. As is the case with airline catering, the mobile module – a trolley – is then used to deliver the trays to the customers at their seats. For lunch and dinner the tray will contain a cold starter, cheese, a pastry, bread, water and wine. Meanwhile, the hot main course will be reheated in a large microwave oven in the small galley located between R1 and R2 and then served. Coffee or tea is heated in the galley. No food is cooked on-board and all plates, glasses and cutlery are loaded back into the modules and washed at the shorebase. Items for the bar, located in R4, are loaded into separate modules. The range includes sandwiches, cakes, several hot items such as toasted sandwiches, burgers and pizzas, and hot and cold drinks. The hot items are reheated in a microwave oven behind the bar.

So far as the train is concerned, the system has a number of advantages. Supplies can be loaded on board just a few minutes before departure and one staff member can serve 20 or more full meals while a second person works the bar; the weight and space required for the galley is minimal compared with a classic train kitchen. Set against this is the high cost of the high-tech supply centres which have been built at Paris Montparnasse and Paris Nord and at other provincial locations. Maintaining the cost of the hygiene chain in the depot and then to the train is costly in equipment and manpower.

Wagon-Lits at-seat meal service in first class on TGV Nord Europe. Under new arrangements from January 1998, Wagon-Lits provides food and beverage services on all French domestic TGV services. *SNCF*

On the whole, TGV catering has been accepted by SNCF clientele, although its perception has a number of negative features. While the quality of food is generally good, there is little scope for on-board flexibility. Passengers are encouraged to book their meals when they buy their travel tickets, but while there may be some meals available for casual customers, there is always the possibility that demand will exceed supply. Because the shelf-life of TGV meal trays is short and valid for only one journey, meals put on for casual sale but not sold have to be wasted. Buffet items have a longer shelf life and can be safely recycled for a second journey.

Another issue is ambience. Whatever the quality of the food and drink, a tray meal on a fold-down table is claustrophobic. Also, because airlines include the meal in the price of the travel ticket, many passengers resent paying FFr 220 for a TGV meal. The value comparison is of course the cost of the air ticket against the cost of a TGV ticket plus the cost of the meal. Meals included in the first class travel ticket are part of the AVE, Eurostar and THALYS offer. Grandes Lignes also offer a complimentary continental breakfast on some TGVs. This arrangement eliminates the uncertainty both for the customer and for the caterer.

Catering on TGVs (and classic SNCF trains) is not provided by the railway, but is awarded to outside catering companies. The contract to supply the Paris Sud Est route when it was launched in 1981 was awarded to Wagon-Lits, Europe's oldest caterer. Servair, the catering affiliate of Air France, won the Atlantique line tender, and Wagon-Lits won the contract for Nord Europe domestic services. In 1993, the Sud Est contract was reassigned from Wagon-Lits to Servair. In 1997, all SNCF train catering contracts were offered for tender, on the basis that a subsidy would no longer be paid by the railway. From January 1998 all TGV catering – with the exception of international services – has been provided by Wagon-Lits who have accepted financial responsibility for the provision of the services and choice of products offered for sale.

Supplying TGVs from Paris Nord is much more complicated. As each of the three services using the Gare du Nord – SNCF domestic, Eurostar and THALYS – has a separate catering contract, it was not possible for each caterer to have its own supply facility. SNCF therefore decided to separate on-board catering from shorebase management which would be covered by a separate contract awarded after competitive tender. Paris Nord shorebase is managed by a separate company – Nordrail – owned 51% by Servair and 49% by Wagons-Lits. Nordrail functions like a supermarket. The on-board caterers order supplies from Nordrail who prepare the modules and deliver them to the trains. They are responsible for preparing and recycling all the on-board equipment such as trays, plates, glass and cutlery etc.

TGV cuisine Italian style. The Italian train catering company AGAPE has the contract to provide food and drink on the Paris – Milan TGV service.
Brian Perren

AVE (Alta Velocita Española)

On 9 December 1988, the Spanish government gave the go-ahead to build the first section – 471 km (293 miles) from Madrid to Seville – of a new high-speed railway to be part of the European high-speed network. Because the line serves Spain's Andalusia region, the railway was originally known as Nouvel Accès Ferroviaire Andalusia (NAFA), but this was subsequently changed to Alta Velocita Española (AVE). Spanish Railways (RENFE) has now adopted AVE as its brand name both for high-speed routes and trains.

The motivation for the new railway was the need to bring Spain's railway network up to standards necessary for a country now looking for economic growth and to create transport infrastructure consistent with Spain's membership of the European Union. While about 50% of RENFE's network was already electrified, albeit at 3 kV dc, about 80% of the network was single-track with numerous operating constraints and bottlenecks. Low track speeds produced uncompetitive journey times.

Another factor inhibiting Spain's rail links with the rest of Europe is track gauge, which is the wider 1.668 rather than the UIC standard 1.435-metre track width used in the rest of Europe including Britain. To a limited extent the gauge problem has been eased by the use of wagons and 'Talgo' passenger coaches with adjustable axles which can travel from France through into Spain, but the axle adjustment – carried out as the train passes through machinery at the border entry point to Spain – takes about 20 minutes.

An important sign that Spain was emerging from decades of political and economic isolation was the technical decision that its new high-speed lines would be built to the standard European UIC 1.435-metre track width. Next, having decided outline plans for a national high-speed network, the hub of which would be the capital city Madrid, the government decided to proceed first with Madrid-Seville rather than Madrid-Barcelona, even though the case for this route was better. Madrid-Seville was relatively easy to build, it would qualify for a 30% EU grant towards the cost of the infrastructure, it would unlock the undeveloped south-west region of the country – and it would be ready in time for the Expo 1992 to be staged in Seville. Also, having built Madrid-Seville, the case for Madrid-Barcelona – including the link-up with the French TGV network – would be irresistible.

Partly to contain cost but also as the line was to be used for classic locomotive-hauled passenger trains and some freight services in addition to purpose-built TGV-style trainsets, the Madrid-Seville line has been constructed with a maximum gradient of 1.25%. Operating speeds are 300 km/h for high-speed trains and 200 km/h for locomotive-hauled 'Talgo 200' trains. The 471 kilometre railway is signalled for two-way working. The catenary design is similar to that used for the German high-speed lines. Because it is designed for mixed-traffic operation, the German LZB (Linien Zug Beinflussung) cab-signalling system was chosen rather than the French TVM system. Control of the line – which allows three-minute headways at 300 km/h or spacing of 12 kilometres between trains – is from a new signalling centre at Madrid Atocha station. Except for the Madrid and Seville station areas, where to facilitate power distribution 3 kV dc has been used, 25 kV ac has been used for the new line.

There are 17 tunnels totalling 15,819 metres and 31 viaducts totalling 9,845 metres. Axle-load is 17 tonnes for TGV-style power cars and 22.5 tonnes for locomotives. Except for two sections – Kilometre 225 to 343 which is 3,200 metres and Kilometre 285 to 318 which is 2,300 metres – minimum radius curves are 4,000 metres.

Madrid to Seville AVE train passes through the Castillan Plateau at KP 266 on the Spanish high-speed line. *Reinhard Douté*

AVE Unit 01 pauses at Cordoba en route from Madrid to Seville. *Reinhard Douté*

Starting at the rebuilt Madrid Puerta de Atocha station – which has seven AVE and eight broad gauge tracks – the new railway runs through the Madrid suburbs for about 10 kilometres, from where it proceeds in open country. At Tage (Kilometre 63) the line begins a long 18-kilometre 1.25% climb to 700 metres above sea level through the Tolède Mountains before descending for the Ciudad Real basin. There is a new combined AVE and broad-gauge station at Ciudad Real. For part of the way from Ciudad Real to the second station at Puertollano (210 kilometres from Madrid) the route is alongside the broad-gauge Manzanares secondary line.

The choice of route from Puertollano to Cordoba (133 kilometres) involved difficult terrain, necessitating four tunnels in varying lengths from 1,200 to 1,700 metres between Kilometre 230 and 255, curvature reduced from 4,000 to 3,200-metre radius involving a speed reduction from 270 to 250 km/h. The second summit of the line, at an altitude of 800 metres, is at Vemta De La Inès Tunnel at Kilometre 247. This is followed by the most difficult section of the line – from Sierra Morena (Kilometre 277) to Cordoba. For 56 kilometres the line descends by 600 metres on a falling gradient averaging 1.09% but with some sections at 1.25%. This entailed construction of 12 viaducts totalling 3,013 metres and nine tunnels totalling 7,088 metres. To minimise construction costs the designers reduced the curve radius over 28 kilometres of this section to 2,300 metres, limiting the maximum speed to 210 km/h.

At Cordoba – 343 kilometres from Madrid and the last of the three intermediate stations on the new railway – RENFE built a new station 500 metres to the west of the old one. From Cordoba the route follows the Guadalquivir River to the end of the line at Seville Santa Justa station, 471 kilometres (293 miles), from Madrid. Santa Justa has six AVE and six broad gauge tracks.

To provide the Madrid-Seville core service RENFE chose a modified version of the French TGV Atlantique trainset; an initial order for 16 trainsets was placed with GEC Alsthom in 1988. Some of these vehicles were built in France, but most of the construction and assembly was undertaken by GEC Alsthom's factories in Barcelona and Valencia.

Whereas the Atlantique trainset has 10 trailers, the AVE has eight in a standard articulated formation enclosed by two power cars. Apart from a slightly different front-end styling, the power cars are the same except that the two voltages are 25 kV ac and 3 kV dc. There are eight 1,100 kW synchronous motors on two motor bogies positioned under the power cars; 25 kV output is 8,800 kW and 3 kV output is 5,400 kW. Train length is 200.19 metres; mass is 392 tonnes empty and 420 tonnes loaded. In December 1993 RENFE placed a second order for a further eight trainsets bringing the AVE fleet up to 24 units. The first two trains in the order have 1.435-metre wheel sets and are used to strengthen the Madrid-Seville route; the other eight have 1.668-metre wheel sets and for the time being they are used to upgrade the classic broad-gauge service between Barcelona and Valencia. In the longer-term they will be fitted with 1.435-metre wheel sets either to further strengthen the Madrid-Seville route or for the Madrid-Barcelona service which will be phased-in from 1998.

Seating layout is based on three travel categories:

- Club: 30 semi-compartment seats, similar to the French Atlantique concept, in coach R1 which also has a small saloon for eight passengers.

- Preferente: 78 2+1 open plan seats in R2 and R3.

- Turista: 213 2+2 open plan facing and uni-directional seats in R5, R6, R7 and R8.

A complete coach – R4 – has been used for a spacious bar car finished in a very stylish décor.

A British design house – Addison – was engaged to produce a distinctive styling for the AVE and other coaches and locomotives in the RENFE high-speed fleet. The external livery is white, blue and grey. As the Spanish market requires a high standard of ambience and luxury, the internal styling of the AVE trains is superior to its French counterparts.

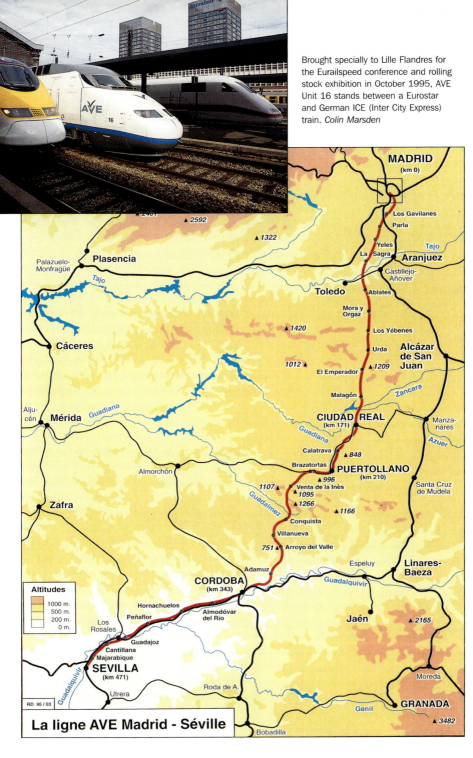

Brought specially to Lille Flandres for the Eurailspeed conference and rolling stock exhibition in October 1995, AVE Unit 16 stands between a Eurostar and German ICE (Inter City Express) train. *Colin Marsden*

MADRID
(km 0)

Los Gavilanes

Parla

Yeles

La Sagra

Tajo

Aranjuez

Castillejo-Añover

Plasencia

Palazuelo-Monfragüe

Tajo

▲ 2592

▲ 1322

Toledo

Ablates

Mora y Orgaz

Los Yébenes

Cáceres

▲ 1420

Urda

Alcázar de San Juan

1012 ▲

El Emperador

▲ *1209*

Zancara

Malagón

Alju-cén

Mérida

Guadiana

Guadiana

CIUDAD REAL
(km 171)

Manza-nares

Azuer

Calatrava

▲ *848*

Brazatortas

PUERTOLLANO
(km 210)

Santa Cruz de Mudela

Almorchón

▲ *996*

1107 ▲

Venta de la Inès

▲ *1095*

Guadalmez

▲ *1266*

▲ *1166*

Zafra

Conquista

Villanueva

751 ▲ Arroyo del Valle

Adamuz

Espeluy

Linares-Baeza

CORDOBA
(km 343)

Guadalquivir

Hornachuelos

Almodóvar del Rio

Peñaflor

Jaén

▲ *2165*

Los Rosales

Guadajoz

Cantillana

Majarabique

SEVILLA
(km 471)

Guadalquivir

Utrera

Roda de A.

Moreda

GRANADA

Genil

▲ *3482*

Bobadilla

Altitudes	
	1000 m.
	500 m.
	200 m.
	0 m.

RD 95 / 03

La ligne AVE Madrid - Séville

Six AVE sets – which have wheelsets for the wider 1,668 metre Spanish gauge – are used for the new EUROMED service between Barcelona, Valencia and Alicante. *Bryan Philpot*

While the AVE buffet vehicle is based on the SNCF Atlantique design, a higher standard of ambience and customer service is on offer. *RENFE*

Although not strictly within the terms of reference for this handbook, mention should be made of the locomotive-hauled Talgo 200 trains which also use the Madrid-Seville line and carry the AVE branding. Clearly, the new railways in Spain would not be justified purely as high-speed links between major centres such as Madrid, Seville and Barcelona. Spain is a large country and the possibility of a general reduction in journey times between the numerous smaller regional towns is very important both economically and socially. A general improvement of inter-city train services from Madrid to places such as Malaga, Cadiz and Huelva was only possible by using dual-gauge 'Talgo' equipment, able to run over the new UIC standard and classic broad-gauge network. Developed by the Talgo[1] company, these trains are formed of low-slung articulated cars with only one axle under each vehicle, but their most significant feature is adjustable bogies. Talgo services have run between Madrid and Paris via Irun and Barcelona and Zürich for some time.

A more recent development is incorporation of a passive tilting system which allows Talgo trains to pass through curves at higher speeds than conventional trains. Gauge changing machinery is now installed at seven locations – Las Matas (Madrid), San Andrés (Barcelona), Port Bou, Irun, Puerta de Atocha (Madrid), Cordoba and Majarabique. Talgo 200 trains are hauled by the new RENFE Class 252 four-axle locomotive, a development of the DB AG Class 120. These locomotives have four 1,400 kW asynchronous traction motors giving a total output of 5,600 kW; they can operate in 25 kV or 3 kV dc mode. Maximum speed is 220 km/h. Fifteen of these locomotives have 1.435-metre wheel sets and the remaining 60 have wide-gauge wheel sets, but they are interchangeable.

With the successful commissioning of the Madrid-Seville line, RENFE and the Spanish government are now proceeding with the various stages of a national railway infrastructure plan. Approved early in 1993, the plan – prepared by the Ministry of Public Works Transport & Environment – includes the upgrading of existing broad-gauge routes as well as new purpose-built lines. So far as high speed is concerned, the priority is a standard European gauge link from Madrid through Zaragoza to Barcelona and thence to the French frontier to link up with the Montpellier leg of TGV Méditerranée. Agreement for this link has been confirmed by an accord signed by the Spanish and French governments. Targeted for completion by 2007, the Spanish government hopes that investment will proceed on an orderly basis irrespective of short-term fluctuations in the national economy.

Work on the 605-kilometre (376-mile) Madrid to Barcelona standard gauge line started in 1994, but as the project will take several years to complete it was necessary to determine a series of priorities, particularly for two critical single-track poorly-aligned sections of route – Clatayud to Ricia and Zaragoza to Lleida – currently operating at saturation levels. Tracklaying, power supplies, signalling and other equipment should be in place by 1998. Although the new route is to be standard gauge, initially dual-gauge track will be installed on these two sections so that some existing broad gauge services can be diverted away from the congested bottleneck sections on the old network. This will enable shorter journey times for a number of existing services and contribute to an early increase in revenue. Thus, the broad-gauge versions of the AVE train and gauge-convertible Talgo 200 trains will be able to use both sections of route. When the project is complete in 2007 RENFE is looking to a 2 hours 30 minutes journey time from Madrid to Barcelona – a *vitesse commerciale* of 242 km/h (145 mph). By this time the next section from Barcelona to the French frontier should be complete, allowing through operation of high-speed services from Seville through Madrid and Barcelona to Paris.

---

[1] Talgo takes its name from Tren Articulado Ligero Goicoechea Oriol; the last two words are the names of the engineers who invented the system.

EUROSTAR

Thanks to the Channel Tunnel, Eurostar high-speed trains routinely run between London (Waterloo International), Paris Nord and Brussels Midi, sometimes without any intermediate stop. Planning and implementation of the Eurostar service has opened up international railway operations on the scale well beyond what was previously the case anywhere in mainland Europe, or indeed the world.

After years of indecision a tunnel linking Britain with Mainland Europe is now a reality. The historic Anglo-French Fixed Link Treaty – which was signed by Prime Minister Margaret Thatcher and President François Mitterrand in Canterbury on 12 February 1986 – opened the way for the century's most exciting railway project.

Eurotunnel's system consists of three separate tunnels – two railway tunnels known as Running Tunnel North (RTN) and Running Tunnel South (RTS) and between them, and linked to them, a Service Tunnel (ST). These three tunnels are just over 50 kilometres (31 miles) long. Eurotunnel's revenue is from two sources – its own dedicated shuttle trains carrying cars, coaches, lorries and passengers between Cheriton (near Folkestone) and Coquelles (near Calais), and from tolls paid by the railways for the passage of international passenger and freight trains under the usage agreement.

Bound for Brussels Midi, this Eurostar has just left the Channel Tunnel and is approaching Calais Fréthun TGV station from where it will accelerate up to the full 300 km/h line speed. *Brian Perren*

Although the tunnel infrastructure is designed for a possible maximum speed of 200 km/h, Eurotunnel's shuttles – Le Shuttle – run to a maximum speed of only 130 km/h (80.8 mph). This gives a terminal-to-terminal transit time of 33 minutes. Maximum speed of passenger trains is 160 km/h (100 mph) and 140 km/h (87 mph) for international freight trains. The official state opening of the Channel Tunnel was held in May 1994, but public services did not start until later that year.

The cross-Channel market is massively larger than it was 30 years ago, but its characteristics are now totally different. In the age of mass travel, expectations are very much higher. Separate research by BR, SNCF and Eurotunnel identified a potential market – given a high-quality service with journey times of 3 hours or less between London and Paris or Brussels – of around 15 million passengers per year for through rail journeys via the Channel Tunnel in addition to Eurotunnel's own separate car and lorry shuttle trains. This was expected to rise to 19.23 million passengers per year by 2000.

There have been significant changes on the British side in the 10 years since the Anglo-French Fixed Link Treaty was signed. British Rail was a single state-owned corporate entity responsible for the operation of its trains and maintenance of its infrastructure. With privatisation, responsibility for infrastructure – signalling, track maintenance and the allocation of train paths – has passed to a new publicly-owned company, Railtrack. European Passenger Services (EPS) – now renamed Eurostar UK Ltd – which was the BR sector responsible for Channel Tunnel passenger services, has now been transferred to London & Continental, the consortium awarded the concession to build the Channel Tunnel Rail Link (CTRL) (Chapter 27). The revenue stream from Eurostar will be used to part-fund the CTRL. These changes have affected the organisational responsibilities for the British side of Eurostar operations.

Many customers use the conveniently-located Ashford International station, opened in January 1996. This service is about to depart for Paris Nord. *Colin Marsden*

Two important items concerning the Eurostar train-service specification are written into the Eurotunnel usage agreement. This specifies that Eurostar UK, SNCF and SNCB will provide a service between London and Paris with a journey time between 2 hours 50 minutes and 3 hours 10 minutes and a 2 hours 40 minutes timing between London and Brussels.

To meet these guarantees – with regard to both speed and frequency – the British, French and Belgian railways initiated massive programmes of infrastructure investment. On the French side, the government had already decided that, if the Channel Tunnel was built, it would go ahead with the TGV Nord Europe. Belgium plans provided for the construction of a new high-speed route from the French frontier to a point close to the centre of Brussels and upgraded infrastructure from there to Brussels Midi terminal station.

At that time there was no proposal for a high-speed line from London through Kent to the Channel Tunnel. Instead it was decided to use existing routes from London to the Tunnel. Even if the CTRL had been politically acceptable, there was no way it could have been designed, planned and funded within the same timescale. BR studies showed that, given the upgrading of the classic routes, it would be possible to superimpose the Eurostar service on a revised commuter timetable without detriment to this politically-sensitive traffic. Both the Tonbridge (Channel Tunnel Route 1: CTR1) and Maidstone East (Channel Tunnel Route 2: CTR2) routes to the Tunnel have been upgraded with new drainage, ballast, rails and enhanced traction current supplies. To provide higher speeds and increased capacity both routes have been resignalled; new junctions have been installed, and track layouts realigned.

Hitherto, continental traffic between London and the Channel ports was handled at Victoria station, but there was neither the space nor the capacity to cope with Eurostar. A superb new award-winning terminal station has been built at Waterloo, necessitating a new connection to link the lines from Kent with the tracks leading into Waterloo International terminal station. While the emphasis for this work has been for Eurostar and Channel Tunnel freight traffic, the commuters of Kent also have a much improved railway. To provide a Eurostar railhead for Kent and South East England there is a new international station at Ashford; this opened in January 1996.

The most challenging part of the train planning process undertaken by timetable specialists in Eurostar UK, Railtrack, Eurotunnel, SNCF and SNCB, is the production of a viable plan consistent with the quite different operating characteristics for each section of Eurostar route. For the first stage – the 71 miles (115 kilometres) from Waterloo International to the UK tunnel entrance (North Portal) – Eurostars use Railtrack infrastructure which they have to share with other users. To meet Eurostar's requirements, four train paths in each direction between Waterloo International and the Tunnel have been allocated, except in the commuter peaks when a reduced number of paths are available. These are sufficient to meet Eurostar's short and medium-term requirements, hopefully up to the time when the CTRL is commissioned. But it is important to note that capacity to cope with long-term growth of commuter traffic, international passenger and freight traffic and not speed *per se* is the main justification for the new route.

As off-peak services in South East London and Kent are organised on a 30-minute clock-face, the four Eurostar paths an hour have been drawn in two pairs with a 4-minute separation with a similar pair 30 minutes later. Because of the importance of the Monday to Friday commuter peak services – more especially in the evening – it has not been possible to offer these paths out of Waterloo International between 1730 and 1830. This restriction follows an undertaking – given by the British Government to local authorities in Kent in order to secure the passage of the Channel Tunnel Bill through Parliament – that international services would not interfere with commuter trains. Given this constraint, the sequence of Eurostar departures from Waterloo in the critical evening peak period – a popular time for returning business travellers to France and Belgium – is less than ideal. A similar constraint applies up to 0930 arrivals in London, but this is less of a problem.

Different circumstances apply for the tunnel transit. While Eurotunnel's own 140 km/h trains will have a 26-minute transit time, a Eurostar at 160 km/h can get through in a little over 19 minutes. As maximum tunnel capacity is only possible if all trains run at equal speed, a Eurotunnel 'Le Shuttle' – or an international freight train running in the same speed band – will consume one standard tunnel path, but a Eurostar on a 160 km/h 21-minute path will consume three standard tunnel paths. Two consecutive Eurostar trains running through the tunnel will use four paths and if three were to run they will consume five paths and so on. Fortunately, the two consecutive 4-minute path formula from Waterloo International to the tunnel enables two consecutive Eurostars to access the tunnel in the most cost-effective way. Tunnel paths inbound from France have been fixed to match as closely as possible the 4-minute spacing over Railtrack infrastructure to Waterloo International.

From the French Portal (South Portal) trains go straight onto TGV Nord Europe. Dedicated to high speed operation with all trains on the same point-to-point timings at speeds up to 300 km/h, with a 3-minute operating headway, pathing is less constrained than on the UK side of the Channel. From the end of the Nord Europe line at Gonesse, Eurostars share classic tracks into the Gare du Nord with SNCF domestic services. For security reasons Eurostar has its own dedicated terminal – Platforms 3 to 6 – known as the 'Gare de Londres'.

Although for many years Victoria was the main London terminus for connecting rail services to the Channel Ports, there was no space to expand the station to cope with the significant increase in passengers expected to use Eurostar services. Instead, a new terminus – Waterloo International – with five dedicated platforms was built alongside the existing domestic station. *Brian Morrison*

With the Belgian high-speed south line now commissioned, Eurostars have a fast route from the Fretin triangle to Brussels Midi, where a dedicated terminal was already in service. Until the new line was opened, from Lille Europe the trains had been using a short single-line connection onto the SNCF classic network, from where they proceeded via Baisieux, Tournai, Ath and Halle to reach Brussels. This was a slow capacity-constrained route which added about 35 minutes to the London-Brussels target journey time. Because of the problems which affected the Eurostar timetable following the Channel Tunnel fire in November 1996 – which restricted tunnel capacity until repair work was completed in May 1997 – some Eurostars between London and Brussels were re-routed via Fretin, Antoing and the classic line through Mons. This route is a few minutes slower.

Waterloo International to Paris Nord is one the fastest inter-city journey-times out of London. Maximum and average speeds from Waterloo International to Portal Nord are much lower than speeds from Portal Sud over TGV Nord Europe to Paris; timings through South East London and Kent are – notwithstanding infrastructure upgrading – quite slow. No other key route out of London has so many permanent speed restrictions before trains can accelerate up to reasonable speeds. Track geometry is such that it takes no less than 19 minutes for a Eurostar leaving Waterloo International to pass Bickley Junction, a distance of just 13 miles. Beyond Orpington the line speed for Eurostars over CTR1 is 80–100 mph, although there is a 50 mph restriction over the curve west of Tonbridge station. Scheduled time from Waterloo International to passing Portal Nord is 70 minutes – average speed 61 mph. The 30-miles (50.5 km) Tunnel transit is 21 minutes, average 88 mph.

Except through Lille, where speeds are reduced to 200 km/h, TGV Nord Europe line speed is 300 km/h to the end of the route at Gonesse. Scheduled times are 25½ minutes pass-to-pass Portal Sud to Lille Europe (245 km/h:152.5 mph), 48½ minutes pass-to-pass Lille Europe to Gonesse (259 km/h:161.1 mph) and 9 minutes from there through to the Gare du Nord. These timings produce a 2 hours 54 minutes schedule from Waterloo International to Paris Nord, a *vitesse commerciale* of 106 mph (170.5 km/h). This is the optimum Waterloo International-Paris Nord schedule; some other non-stop trains are allowed a few extra minutes for pathing purposes. Some trains also make calls at Ashford International, Calais-Fréthun TGV and Lille Europe, but no train will make more than two intermediate stops; journey time with two intermediate stops is a little over 3 hours.

Timings for the Brussels service are the same between Waterloo International and Lille Europe. For the present a time of 1 hour 11/12 minutes is in force over the Tournai route from Lille Europe to Brussels Midi. From December 1997 a time of 2 hours 35 minutes between Waterloo International and Brussels Midi is envisaged.

Until the Channel Tunnel Rail Link opens around 2003, Eurostars will remain on the classic route from Waterloo International to the Channel Tunnel through South East London and Kent. Although the route has been upgraded, the alignment is such that reasonably good speeds are not possible until several miles out of London. This Eurostar is passing through Brixton where there is a 45 mph speed restriction. *Brian Perren*

Learning the road. Eurostars are driven by a cadre of international drivers who are fluent in at least two languages and must be familiar with every detail of the route between London, Brussels and Paris. Part of their training is undertaken in the Eurostar simulator, but this is also supplemented by road-learning journeys in a specially adapted train, with the seats arranged like a theatre, so that the trainees can observe every part of the track ahead. This group of drivers is from Britain, France and Belgium. *Brian Perren*

Launch of Eurostar was a unique railway event posing quite different challenges to those previously encountered by the participating railways. Every component of the service – the trains (considered to be the most technically complicated ever designed), the routes, bilingual and trilingual train crews, and of course the tunnel itself – was new.

A potential traffic of 15 million single Eurostar journeys a year between the UK, France and Belgium was the basis for the purchase of 38 trainsets and for a timetable plan with 41 services in each direction. Timescales for the expansion of the service will depend on the rate of growth in the next few years.

Density of traffic between London and the tunnel is such that paths for Eurostars cannot be changed without a major revision to other services using the route. While the UK end is the most inflexible part of the timetable, planning for other locations is by no means easy. Other constraints include the timing of connections at Lille Europe with SNCF's domestic TGVs to other parts of France and the 'white period'. As SNCF prefers to undertake certain essential infrastructure inspections only in daylight hours, most trunk routes have a gap in the timetable – the 'white period' – when no trains can run. This gap is 70 minutes on the Nord Europe line. Good connections between Eurostar arrivals/departures at Brussels Midi with THALYS TGVs for the Netherlands and Germany are another feature which has to be considered.

There are two intermediate stations – Ashford International and Calais-Fréthun TGV between London and Lille Europe, each of which costs five minutes running time. Consequently, the choice of calls by two consecutive trains has to be carefully managed. When a pair of outbound trains call at Ashford International, the second train will use the standard path to Ashford and will arrive at the tunnel five minutes later than normal. Inbound trains calling at Ashford will pass through the tunnel five minutes earlier than usual and take up a normal path from Ashford.

When Channel Tunnel legislation was passing through Parliament, there was concern that the tunnel would only benefit London and South East England. To reassure MPs from the English regions, Wales and Scotland, the Government directed BR to prepare plans for passenger (and freight) services to points beyond London. This exhortation – set out in Section 40 of the Channel Tunnel Act – subsequently passed to Eurostar UK Ltd, a subsidiary of London & Continental Railways (see Chapter 27). Politically the concept of through trains from Paris and Brussels to UK provincial destinations was very attractive, but within railway circles there were doubts about the viability of these services, particularly since Section 42 of the Channel Tunnel Act specifically forbade any Government subsidy for international passenger and freight services. Nonetheless, as mentioned in Chapter 11, an order was placed for seven Eurostar trainsets adapted to work over the UK East and West Coast main lines. Unfortunately, the launch of these services – now referred to as Regional Eurostar – was seriously delayed by technical problems caused by possible traction current interference with track circuits and the consequent effect on signalling and safety.

Even if Railtrack's go-ahead had been obtained, there were by the end of 1997 serious doubts about commercial viability. Given the distances involved, journey times would have been quite long. Paris to Manchester would have been around 6 hours and Paris-Glasgow around 9 hours 25 minutes – hardly likely to generate sufficient business to fill each 558-seat train throughout the year. Accordingly, towards the end of 1997, Eurostar UK began to look at other revenue-earning options for the deployment of these expensive high-tech trainsets. At the time of writing, Eurostar was in negotiation with Virgin Trains for the possible leasing of the seven Regional Eurostar trainsets for use between London (Euston) and Manchester Piccadilly starting in May 1999. The trains would retain their Eurostar branding and would be operated by Eurostar crews. If agreed, this arrangement will enable Virgin Trains to make a significant improvement to its West Coast services pending delivery of its new fleet of tilting trains expected to be in service by 2001-2. By this time the Channel Tunnel Rail Link should be open enabling – in combination with the upgrading of the UK West Coast main line – attractive journey times from Paris and Brussels to Birmingham and Manchester.

It was clear from the outset that an efficient and cost-effective operation would only be achieved by joint management of trainsets and train crews. For corporate accounting purposes ownership of the 31 Capitals trainsets is 11 Eurostar UK, 16 SNCF and 4 SNCB, while the 7 Regional Eurostar trainsets are all owned by Eurostar UK. Each of the 38 trainsets will normally be maintained at its home depot – Eurostar UK at North Pole International, SNCF at Le Landy (Paris) and SNCB at Forest (Brussels). But to get the most effective daily utilisation, there will be occasions where a trainset programme concludes at an 'away' station. In these cases overnight routine maintenance will be undertaken at the location depot. Also, with joint management of spare parts – traction motors, door units, pantographs etc – equipment failures will be rectified at the nearest location depot irrespective of ownership.

Security and operational safety are paramount. To ensure no unauthorised person has access to the trains, depots and stations are fully protected by most stringent security measures. For security – but also for customer care and yield management purposes – a compulsory reservation system applies, and access to the trains is only possible through the automated check-in system at the main stations. Strict controls will also apply at the UK regional stations where Eurostar passengers will join.

In preparation for the now postponed Glasgow to Paris service Regional Eurostar Unit 3308/7 makes a test visit to verify the gauging at Glasgow Central. *Colin Marsden*

Eurostars have been designed to comply with the safety procedures set by the inter-governmental safety commission for Channel Tunnel operation. Each trainset consists of four elements – two power cars and two nine-car (seven for Regional Eurostar) half-sets. In the event of failure or another emergency the train can be uncoupled and a half-set driven out of the tunnel independently with all passengers from the train aboard.

For safety purposes, a minimum of seven train crew is required for the tunnel transit. If a half-train evacuation within the tunnel is required, the driver will remain at the front of the train and another suitably qualified person will go to the rear cab. Each of the two train managers will be in charge of their respective half-sets and will be assisted by cater-ing staff if evacuation of passengers into the service tunnel is necessary. Train managers' other duties include customer care and revenue protection activities.

Day-to-day supervision is undertaken by an international control office – *Centre de Côntrole Voyageurs* (CCV) – located in Lille. CCV is part of an international control group whose duties include freight as well as passenger traffic and liaison with Eurotunnel.

At an early planning stage the railway partners concluded that on business, operational and productivity grounds, the service would best function if the same crew worked throughout the entire journey. Stopping en route just to change train crews adds extra minutes to the journey which must be as short as possible to give the service competitive edge. An intermediate crew change introduces a potential source of delay into the opera-tion. If a Eurostar is delayed at the beginning of its journey, a situation could develop when a train does not get to the changeover point in time for the driver to take over his return working. The delay is then extended to two trains, affecting both directions of travel rather than containing it to one.

Notwithstanding difficulties of culture and national working practices, the three rail-ways have established a *cadre* of high-calibre bilingual drivers capable of working the core Capitals routes. Eurostar UK drivers were recruited from BR. SNCF has selected drivers from La Chapelle (Paris), Fives (Lille) and Fréthun (Calais); SNCB has selected drivers from Brussels, Antwerp and Liège. This says a great deal for the quality of the people involved that British drivers (the British are not noticeably good at languages) can take a Eurostar non-stop to Paris or Brussels into what a few years ago would have been consid-ered alien territory. Likewise the French and Belgian drivers have had to grapple with English plus the third-rail network through Kent and South East London involving a very high number of low-speed junctions and alternative route permutations.

Given the particular characteristics of the Eurostar market – hitherto dominated by the airlines – the three railway partners adopted a completely new marketing approach. Although the trains run over three national railway systems plus Eurotunnel, customers are offered an homogenous product identified by the distinct Eurostar branding. While staff have been recruited in Britain, France and Belgium, at least half of the passengers will at any time be outside their own country. Thus, all Eurostar staff – both those receiv-ing passengers at stations and on-board the trains – have to speak both English and French, plus Flemish for those services to Belgium. All staff – including drivers – have dis-tinctive uniforms designed by Pierre Balmain.

On-board catering and customer care is an essential part of the Eurostar offer. Catering is provided by Cross Channel Catering Company (CCCC), a consortium formed by Wagons-Lits, the European Rail Catering Company (previously BR InterCity) and Sabena. The style of service is derived from the TGV concept based on airline-style tray meals, with hot courses regenerated on-board, a take-away service from each of the two train bars, and sales trolleys throughout standard class. In first class the meal of the hour – including drinks and coffee – is included in the price of the ticket. A full Eurostar catering team con-sists of 16 staff, two of whom are trained for tunnel evacuation procedures. Food ordering and train staffing can normally be predicted in advance, but there is need for some flexi-bility to cope with a last minute influx of passengers. CCCC keeps a 'top-up' stock of sup-plies on the departing platform which can be loaded on to the train up to the final minutes before departure.

As the service frequency was increased business on the London-Paris route soon grew to the extent that Eurostar is now the firmly-established market leader. Initially it was thought that 60% of the business would be through Paris and 40% through Brussels, whereas the actual split is 75% Paris and 25% Brussels. The slow response in the Brussels market was undoubtedly due to the late commissioning of the Belgian high-speed line to the centre of Brussels (see Chapter 7). Eurostar arrivals and departures at Brussels Midi as being integrated with the new THALYS service to give a range of improved journey opportunities to Liége and Cologne (Köln); changing time at Brussels Midi between the two services will be around 20 minutes.

Having launched the core Three Capitals and Regional Eurostar services, the railway partners have been looking to destinations beyond London, Paris and Brussels. Identifying markets beyond Paris and Brussels is more complex. There are two issues – finding a destination which can justify an 18-car train with 770 seats, and technical constraints concerning traction current supplies. To access possible destinations beyond Paris, Eurostar has to be equipped to work with 1.5 kV dc power supplies. Four trains now have this.

There are, however, niche market opportunities. The first of these – a service to Marne-le-Vallée for the Disneyland Paris – was launched in summer 1996. Aimed at the leisure market, business was such that the service was retained during winter weekends and throughout the summer season and is now a regular Eurostar destination.

Winter sports is a similar leisure opportunity. Around 200,000 British – 25% of the total market – travel to ski resorts in the Tarentaise valley in the French Alps. Most of these holidaymakers buy air-coach packages or go by car. On the face of things air would seem to be a preferable choice, but although passengers get to Geneva or Lyon Satalos Airports quite quickly, they are then faced with a three to four-hour coach journey to reach the ski resort. Although some coach travel will still be necessary, the Eurostar journey from London to the ski resort will be around nine hours – eight hours to Bourg-St-Maurice plus 45 minutes by bus. With stops at both Moutiers and Bourg-St-Maurice, Eurostar will provide a hassle-free journey to some of the world's best ski areas. The service will run in each direction every Saturday from mid-December to early April.

Waterloo International – Paris Nord: Running Times

	Distance		Running Time		Average Speed	
	Km	Miles	Hr	Min	Km/h	Mph
Waterloo International – British Tunnel Portal	114.5	71.1	1	10	98	60.9
Channel Tunnel	50.5	31.4	0	21	144	89.7
French Tunnel Portal – Lille Europe	104.2	64.7	0	26	240	149.3
Lille Europe – Gonesse	209.6	130.2	0	48	262	162.8
Gonesse – Paris Nord	15.8	9.8	0	9	105	65.3
Total	**494.6**	**307.3**	**2**	**54**	**170.5**	**106**

Waterloo International – Brussels Midi: Running Times

	Distance		Running Time		Average Speed	
	Km	Miles	Hr	Min	Km/h	Mph
Waterloo International – British Tunnel Portal	114.5	71.1	1	10	98	60.9
Channel Tunnel	50.5	31.4	0	21	144	89.7
French Tunnel Portal – Lille Europe	104.2	64.7	0	26	240	149.3
Lille Europe – Brussels Midi via Tourrai and Ath	107	66.5	1	14	87	53.9
Total	**376.2**	**233.7**	**3**	**11**	**118**	**73.4**

Commencing in December 1997, a through Eurostar began running in each direction between Waterloo International and Bourg-St-Maurice on Saturdays during the winter sports season. Because of the gradients and curvature on the Bourg-St-Maurice branch, a series of preliminary tests with a Eurostar was undertaken in November 1996. Four Eurostar sets have been modified to operate with 1.5 kV dc power supplies, necessary to access part of the route to the French Alps. Taken during one of the test trips, this Eurostar is rounding the long steeply-graded curve at Landry, the last station before Bourg-St-Maurice. *Phillippe Morel*

Journey Times from Waterloo International

	Time		Vitesse Commerciale		Vitesse Commerciale	
	Hr	Min	Miles	Mph	Kms	Km/h
Calais Fréthun	1	33	104.7	67.5	168	108
Lille Europe	1	59	167.3	84.4	269	136
Paris Nord	2	54	307.3	106.0	495	171
Brussels Midi*	2	34	233.9	91.13	376	146.5

*Via completed Belgian high-speed line to Brussels from December 1997.

21

THALYS

Paris-Brussels-Köln (Cologne)-Amsterdam (PBKA) is a long established rail market, particularly for business travellers between Paris and Brussels. By the early 1970s Paris-Brussels business was sufficient to justify six Trans Europe Express (TEE) first-class services with full dining facilities, plus several two-class classic trains. But by the early 1980s intensified competition from airlines and from the expanded *autoroute* network had severely eroded rail's market share. Even though the non-stop journey between Paris Nord and Brussels Midi was around 2 hours 25 minutes and quicker than car for centre-to-centre city journeys, car was the preferred choice for many travellers.

Today, the total multi-modal traffic on the PBKA axis is around 21 million people, of whom 3.2 million travel by train. By far the largest share of this market is held by the private car (66%), air share is 6%, long-distance bus 10% and rail 15%. Multi-modal traffic between Paris and various points in Belgium is 5 million people per year; market shares are 5% air, 8% long-distance bus, 24% rail and 59% private car. Rail has around 1.2 million passengers per year.

TGV has revolutionised this market. Given the experience elsewhere – particularly Paris–Lyon – the railways expect to generate additional business as well as to gain market share as the new stages of the European High-Speed Network are opened for service. On the Paris–Brussels/Antwerp/Liège section of the PBKA market, SNCF and SNCB aim to increase market share from the present 24% to 51% by 1998 and 60% by 2005.

Two TGV types have the THALYS styling and livery – the 4-voltage PBKA on the left and the 3-voltage PBA on the right of the picture taken in Le Landy depot. *Regis Chessum*

As explained in Chapter 16, new structures for the management of international services have been put in place. For PBKA, SNCF and SNCB set up a joint-venture co-operative company – Westrail International – located in Brussels. In the early stages most of the traffic will be between Paris and stations in Belgium, so initially only SNCF and SNCB are involved with Westrail, but the company structure is such that German (DB AG) and Netherlands Railways (NS) can join at a later stage, probably when the Belgian high-speed line is operational beyond Brussels to the German and Netherlands borders. Westrail is responsible for all high-speed rail business between France and Belgium including the development of Jonction services from Brussels to the South East, South West and Western France.

Before the creation of Westrail, development of business plans such as train service frequency and schedule proposals, pricing strategy, on-board issues, branding and logos, other marketing matters and financial results was pursued through the separate SNCF, SNCB, DB AG and NS management hierarchies – a time-consuming process. The service beyond Brussels is negotiated by Westrail with DB AG and NS. The new organisation has made good progress.

Now that the European high-speed network is beginning to take shape, national brandings such as Inter-City or TGV are not necessarily suitable for specific cross-frontier high-speed markets. TGV is not a suitable branding for a service into Britain, Germany or the Netherlands. *Train à grande vitesse* – TGV – might be suitable for the Belgian Walloons but not so for the Flemish. EPS (now Eurostar UK), SNCF and SNCB were the first to address this issue, which they resolved by choosing Eurostar for the cross-channel high-speed service.

Given the challenge of launching a new high-quality product into a market served by the old-style TEE trains, the quality of which had somewhat faded, the PBKA partners engaged a Belgian-Dutch company – Total Design – to produce a brand name, external livery, logo and internal design for the trainset, although the external shape and profile of both the Réseau and PBKA trainsets had already been determined by Roger Tallon in his role as SNCF's TGV design guru. The external styling is a combination of soft forms of red and metallic grey. The new brand name – THALYS – was chosen for its evocation of speed, comfort and modernity; the logo is intended to depict the displacement of air by an object moving at high speed – a lance in flight towards its target. THALYS has no literal meaning, but is phonetically acceptable in French, German and Dutch (Flemish).

Afternoon THALYS service leaves Amsterdam Central for Paris Nord.
Colin Marsden

Following market research, two important factors influenced the THALYS product – the need to raise the quality of the second class accommodation and to modify the on-board service style in first class. The traditional designation of first and second class has been replaced by Confort 1 and Confort 2. As can be seen from the pictures, the same colours have – for the first time – been used throughout the train. For the interiors, two shades of red have been chosen. Metallic purple was chosen to match the red seats of Confort 1 and metallic blue-green was chosen for Confort 2. The unified THALYS corporate identity is to be used for on-train and station signing and ticketing, timetables and other documentation.

While the old TEEs were noted for the quality of their restaurant and bar service, passengers' tastes have changed, and the drastically reduced journey times by high-speed trains have reduced the need for traditional-style train meals. With the prospect of a 1 hour 25 minute journey-time between Paris and Brussels it was clear that a new catering specification would be necessary. In the preliminary market research referred to earlier, customers expressed a preference for more customer care and less expensive catering to be included in the ticket price.

In Confort 1 food and beverage service is included in the fare; customers will be served at-seat from a trolley. Confort 2 passengers will be served from a bar/buffet which will operate on all trains and on all routes. Following a tender invitation, THALYS catering contract has been awarded to Railmaster, a consortium now comprising Servair, and Rail Gourmet. Railmaster uses the existing shorebases (*Centre d'avitaillement* – CAV) at Paris Nord and Brussels Midi and a third base is under construction at Amsterdam. Confort 1 service has been awarded on the basis of financial support from Westrail International and HST-VCH (the NS high-speed rail subsidiary) for journeys in The Netherlands. The bar service has been awarded as a concession.

Because construction of the Belgian high-speed line to the centre of Brussels has been delayed, the THALYS timetable has been developed in stages. In January 1995 three of the former TEE services were replaced by Réseau TGVs using TGV Nord Europe as far as Lille Europe where, following reversal, the trains continued into Belgium via Baisieux and Tournai. Because of the time taken to reverse at Lille Europe and low line speeds on the Baisieux route, journey time was only marginally better than the classic TEE service via Mons.

From June 1996 – with the opening of the first 15 kilometres of the Belgian high-speed line from the French Frontier to Antoing – the journey time over the 357 kilometres from Paris Nord to Brussels Midi was reduced from 2 hours 21 minutes to 2 hours 3 minutes – a *vitesse commerciale* of 172.5 km/h (107 mph). This was subsequently reduced to 1 hour 57 minutes from September 1996. Until December 1997, THALYS trains left the high-speed line by a single-track connection at Antoing continuing thence to Brussels by way of Mons and Halle. Twenty-seven THALYS trains – 14 from Paris 13 to Paris – are timetabled over the Antoing single-track connection.

Four services in each direction were introduced between Paris Nord and Amsterdam Central with a journey-time of 4 hours 50 minutes. These replaced the four Paris–Amsterdam classic trains, including the EuroCity 'Etoile du Nord', the last service formed with the old TEE equipment. Journeys on the Paris–Amsterdam axis were reduced by an average of 72 minutes. Also, to tap the wider Belgian market, two pairs of THALYS trains were extended to/from Liège together with a late-evening service to and an early morning service from Antwerp Central.

For THALYS the traditional designation of first and second class has been replaced by Confort 1 and Confort 2. The same colour theme has been used throughout the train. All seats are red, contrasted with metallic purple in Confort 1 and blue/grey in Confort 2. *Colin Marsden*

With the completion of the southern section of the Belgian high-speed line from Antoing to Lembeek and the 200 km/h upgrading from there to the final approaches to Brussels Midi at Forest, a significant number of train service improvements were introduced from Sunday 14 December 1997. There will be 18 trains from Paris Nord to Brussels Midi with a 1 hour 25 minute non-stop journey-time, *vitesse commerciale* 215.7 km/h (134 mph). Departures from Paris Nord will be on a clockface system at XX55 past each hour from 0655 to 2055, with a later service at 2128; there will be three extra services at XX25. There will be 17 services from Brussels Midi to Paris Nord mostly at XX40 but with additional departures at XX10 to give a half-hourly service at peak times. Two of the Paris Nord-Brussels Midi clockface trains in each direction will go forward to and start from Ostend calling at Bruges and Gent and one other service in each direction will run forward to and start from Antwerp Central. THALYS has been an immediate success, achieving a 65% average occupancy over the Paris-Brussels section.

Except for the external livery and internal décor, this THALYS end-vehicle built by De Dietrich is the same as the Réseau and PBKA series. *De Dietrich*

For the present the Paris Nord – Amsterdam Central service remains at four trains in each direction, but with sufficient four-voltage PBKA THALYS sets ready for action, there will be seven direct services in each direction between Paris Nord, Brussels Midi–Liège and Köln (Cologne). These will form part of the Paris Nord–Brussels Midi clockface; in some cases they will run as a two-unit combined Paris Nord–Amsterdam, Paris Nord–Köln (Cologne) service which will divide/combine at Brussels Midi. Journey times between Paris Nord and Amsterdam Central will be reduced to 4 hours 25 minutes; journey times between Paris Nord and Köln will be 4 hours 3 minutes.

There will be further journey time reductions to Köln (Cologne) and Amsterdam, the planning of which will depend on timescales for the completion of the Belgian high-speed line beyond Brussels to the German and Netherlands borders and the completion of the Netherlands South Line as described in Chapter 28. Long-term journey-time aspirations are around 3 hours from Paris to Köln (Cologne) and Amsterdam, probably around 2005.

THALYS service at Brussels Midi. *SNCB/NNBS.*

22 TGV POST AND PARCELS

Although the French TGV network is primarily a high-speed passenger system, there is scope to carry light freight traffic – such as post and small parcels – provided the train is within the 17-tonne maximum axle-load limit.

When the PSE project was taking shape, the French Post Office (PTT) – more usually referred to as LA POSTE – recognised that TGV journey times could be a cost-effective addition to its multi-modal distribution network. An agreement was reached whereby the PTT would finance the construction of 2fi purpose-built trainsets for the carriage of mail, and for the construction of a private siding to connect a new postal station with the TGV line just south of Mâcon-Loché TGV station.

The postal TGV service started on 1 October 1984, replacing an overnight air service between Paris and Lyon previously provided by two Transoll 160 aircraft. The payload of a postal TGV is 88 tonnes compared with 14.3 tonnes on the Transoll 160.

Originally there were two daytime and two night services in each direction between Paris Charolais postal depot, located alongside the Gare-de-Lyon, and Lyon Montrochet postal depot, located close to Lyon Perrache passenger station. The two night services both called at Mâcon postal station to exchange mail; these trains were part of the complex distribution network covering the whole of South East France involving air, road and other SNCF services. For direct access to Lyon Montrochet postal station the overnight north and southbound postal TGVs used the PLM line between Creches sur-Saône and Lyon Montrochet to avoid reversal en route. This pattern of service operated for 10 years until it was completely revised from November 1994.

Afternoon postal service from Cavaillon to Paris near Lapalud south of Montélimar. *Michael Collins*

Partly because of the cost of replacing its ageing fleet of classic letter-sorting coaches, but also because mechanised letter-sorting is so much more efficient, the PTT decided to completely revamp its distribution arrangements in South East France. This coincided with the opening of the Rhône Alpes TGV extension offering substantially reduced transit time between Paris and points south of Valence. Accordingly, PTT decided to open a major postal distribution depot at Cavaillon in Provence. Chosen because of its proximity to the A7 autoroute and other major roads, and its position on the 66-km (41-miles) SNCF loop line from Avignon to Miramas, the location was ideal for a major transhipment depot. Letters, parcels and light package traffic from a wide area to/from Paris is now taken to or from Cavaillon by road to the new PTT depot, where it is transferred to either of two new daily TGV services.

The train service now provides for two return services between Paris Charolais and Cavaillon and two each way between Charolais and Mâcon PTT stations. In principle, PTT TGVs are timed to run with their passenger counterparts at the full 270 km/h line speed, but because of maintenance work some early morning and night trains have extended timings.

Because it would not have been possible to cover the increased PTT services with only two operational trainsets an additional set has been made available. To provide the additional unit, SNCF converted PSE Unit 38 – one of the nine first class passenger sets – into a postal train. Converted at Bishheim Works, the set is basically the same as the other postal trains. Because the PTT trains use the Rhône Alpes TGV extension all power cars in the PTT fleet have been equipped with TVM 430 cab-signalling.

To provide cover for maintenance, the 3½ postal sets are numbered in half-sets from one to seven, but they can only operate in the conventional power car, eight-articulated trailers, power car formation. A half-set cannot operate on its own. Changeover of half-sets can only be undertaken at Villeneuve Depot in Paris, where the whole eight-car articulated rake has to be lifted from its bogies and the half-set removed and replaced with the changeover set.

Each afternoon the Cavaillon-Paris Charollais postal train calls at Mâcon postal station to collect mail for Paris. Trolleys of mail are delivered by road and loaded into the train during its brief 20 minute stop. Mâcon postal station is located on a short single-track branch just south of Mâcon-Loché TGV station. *Brian Perren*

The success of the SNCF-PTT collaboration has encouraged SNCF to look at the wider European market for the fast transit of time-sensitive high-value letters and packages. Within the next few years TGV journey times between many major European centres will be significantly reduced – London to Paris could be around 2½ hours, Brussels to Paris will be about 1 hour 20 minutes and Frankfurt to Paris less than 4 hours. At present this market is dominated by a few well-known international freight carriers using a combination of road and air transport. If the market continues to expand, the increasing number of players and rising costs of both air and road transport could erode profit margins. Air space is now more congested, access to airport facilities is more difficult and, further moves to curtail night flights are likely. Also, from 1994 there is a restriction of 110 km/h for lorries weighing 10–12 tonnes and 130 km/h for lorries of less than 10 tonnes.

A series of studies by SNCF suggests that many of the leading freight transport operators would be prepared to switch their business from air and/or road to rail provided very strict quality criteria were guaranteed. Operators would be looking for safety, reliability with ability to perform in those adverse weather conditions which affect air and road transport, and a favourable price reflecting the time, cost and volume of business on offer.

The project being developed by SNCF envisages the creation of a network of freight TGVs running through the night at speeds in the 270–300 km/h range. Based on the Duplex design, the new trains would carry up to 40 ten-metre containers, totally around 100 tonnes of cargo per train. Space on these trains would be sold to carriers, who would check their containers on a destination-to-destination basis. Thus, a container leaving London around 2100 in the late evening would – with a change of train at one of the key modal points in the network – be delivered in Marseille by 0400 on the following morning. The key nodal points in the network – essentially a hub-and-spoke operation – would be served by a series of tightly-timed trains operating to a regular disciplined timetable. While the location of these nodal terminal points will be agreed in association with SNCF's international partners, preliminary studies suggest that a terminal near Charles-de-Gaulle Airport in Paris would be an essential part of the network. The large number of containers going out from or arriving into Charles-de-Gaulle Airport for onward transfer to rail-fed destinations would be a natural tie-up between air and rail.

Given that the commercial offer will be based on fast transits between 2100 and 0400, covering distances between 600 and 1,300 kilometres, overnight access to high-speed lines will be essential. At present SNCF TGV lines are normally closed during the night hours so that routine maintenance can be undertaken, although more prolonged closures will become necessary as the older lines become due for major refurbishment, as is the case with the southern section of the Paris Sud Est line. This is a constraint which will have to be addressed.

Artist's impression of how a TGV Duplex-style train could be adapted as a high-speed freight train: TGV FRET. Note the space potential offered by the Duplex profile. *SNCF*

TGV OPERATIONS

The commercial success of TGV owes much to the production side of SNCF (Direction du Transport) who convert the aspirations of the business side of the organisation (Direction Grandes Lignes) into robust and viable operating plans. This work is based on three objectives: design of a train service which meets customer expectations with regard to journey times, frequency and pricing; creation of conditions for the implementation of operating systems and monitoring day-to-day performance; and the meeting of very strict safety criteria.

Development of the TGV network goes far beyond the task of building a new line and ordering a fleet of high-speed trainsets. The system is not a self-contained operation but has been designed so that TGVs can use the high-speed line to access the entire network, provided the routes are electrified. So, in addition to the investment in high-speed lines and new trainsets, a parallel programme of major works was implemented to adapt key parts of the existing classic network to cope with the greatly increased density of traffic. The classic Paris terminal stations – Gare-de-Lyon, Montparnasse and Paris Nord – have been virtually rebuilt. Passenger amenities have been expanded and enhanced to cope with increased numbers and higher customer expectations and to create the right image for a high-quality contemporary transport product. To maximise trainset utilisation, track layouts and platforms have been modified so that incoming TGVs can be prepared for a return journey in the same platform. New train servicing and maintenance depots have been built.

Bercy Conflans – located just outside the Gare de Lyon – is the main servicing centre for the PSE fleet. At any time there may be as many as 50 sets in the extensive sidings not all of which are in the picture. Incoming trains from the Sud Est can be cleaned and returned to the Gare-de-Lyon for another outward trip within two hours. *Regis Chessum*

PSE heavy maintenance is undertaken at EIMM Villeneuve-St-Georges. An eight-car articulated rake is lifted for bogie changing. *Regis Chessum*

Before describing operations in greater detail, some general points would be helpful. Because the population of France is thinly spread over a large geographical area, there are only four major conurbations – Lille, Paris Ile-de-France, Lyon and Marseille. There are other important centres in France – Nice, Bordeaux, Nantes, Rennes, Grenoble and Strasbourg – but these are comparatively small. Moreover, the distance between the major centres is quite considerable. Paris to Lyon is 270 miles and Lyon to Marseille is 220 miles. Lille to Lyon is 410 miles. In contrast, Paris to Lille is only 140 miles. Another important factor is that most traffic flows in France (road as well as rail) tend to radiate from Paris, although cross-country connections have been improved.

Railways exist to move people (or freight) and the first consideration must always be the market. Given a population spread which is relatively thin, TGV traffic flows vary to a considerable extent. With the exception of Paris-Lyon and Paris–Lille, most long-distance French markets cannot support a regular-interval hourly (or half-hourly) clockface frequency across the country as is the case in more densely-populated countries such as Britain, Belgium, the Netherlands, Germany and Switzerland. Instead many points on the TGV network have only five or six trains a day to/from Paris. Grenoble is a case in point. To cover these markets in the most cost-effective way, services are designed to take the maximum number of passengers to groups of stations in block loads. Concentrating traffic flows in this way enables trains to run from Paris for considerable distances before making their first intermediate stop, thereby minimising journey times.

Another general point is peak demand. Because land is relatively cheap in France, many French families of comparatively modest means own a second home in the provinces, and many have strong roots in the country. These are the reasons for the widespread popularity of '*le weekend*'. While some trains have higher fares on Friday afternoons and Sunday evenings, a significant reserve capacity – particularly trainsets – is retained to meet these peak periods.

The busiest days of the year – not just for TGV but for most of the network – are the Saturdays from the end of December to the end of April for the annual winter sports holiday; and the Saturdays from mid-July to the end of August for summer holidays.

Paris Sud Est

A major programme of associated works was undertaken for the 1981 Paris Sud Est project – the most important of which was the reorganisation of the Gare-de-Lyon terminal station in Paris. Between 1980 and 1982 the layout was completely changed. A new four-platform sub-surface station for suburban trains was built under the old arrival side, releasing space for new TGV platforms. This was also part of a long-term project to join the Sud Est and Nord suburban routes to form RER Line D; this was completed in June 1996 when the tunnel from the Gare-de-Lyon to Châtelet-les-Halles was commissioned.

Part of the 1981 works was the construction of the two maintenance centres at Bercy Conflans and Villeneuve-St-Georges. Located just outside the Gare-de-Lyon on the arrivals side, Bercy Conflans undertakes train cleaning and routine maintenance; extensive sidings are capable of holding up to 50 TGV trainsets. Facilities include inspection pits and automatic washing equipment. The location is such that trains can be taken out to Bercy and returned to the Gare-de-Lyon for another journey within two hours. Located approximately 14 kilometres (8 miles) from the Gare-de-Lyon the Villeneuve-St-Georges facility – *Establissement Industriel de Maintenance du Matéreil* (EIMM) – is the major maintenance base for the PSE fleet; work undertaken includes traction motor, transformer and bogie changes.

EIMM Paris Sud Est: Trainset Allocation		
PSE Two Class	87	
PSE First Class	7	
PSE Three Voltage	9	
PSE Postal	3½	
Réseau Two Voltage	11	
Réseau Three Voltage	6	[1]
Duplex	5	[2]
Total	**128½**	

[1] For Paris–Milan service
[2] Under construction; 30 on order

Above: TGV Ski. Two-unit PSE formation rounds the curve at Landry on the Bourg-St-Maurice branch with a Sunday service conveying passengers for winter holidays in the Alpes. This double Réseau unit has come from Paris and is bound for Bourg-St-Maurice. *Brian Perren*

The busiest days at the Gare-de-Lyon are Fridays throughout most of the year, the days preceding public holidays and the Saturdays between Christmas and the end of April during the annual trek to the Alpes for ski holidays. The super-peaks are the start of the July holidays and the following Saturdays in July and August and the ski peaks on Saturdays in February. For normal business travel the busiest period is Monday to Friday between 0615 and 0815 when 12 important business trains are despatched. From 0800 the activity of the station switches to the arrival side when a group of 12 TGVs from the provinces are scheduled to arrive by 0930. Thus another aspect of TGV capacity is the ability of the station facilities – Metro, RER, taxis, buses, cars, buffets, shops and ticket selling points – to handle the passage of these people.

Platform occupation is the critical factor at the Gare-de-Lyon. On the face of things, 26 platforms – which are also used by longer-distance commuter trains and locomotive-hauled services to points on the old (PLM) line to Dijon and to Clermont Ferrand – would seem to be sufficient for the level of service. About 25 minutes is required to empty and check out an incoming train before it can go empty to Bercy Conflans sidings. Allowing a margin for late running, this means that each platform can cope with two arrivals per hour; two departures an hour is also possible. On this basis it would not be possible to handle 12 TGVs per hour – plus other services – for other than short bursts of activity. Another issue is the ability of the reception sidings at Bercy to receive and process trains through the depot. Careful planning of the Gare-de-Lyon station working is therefore an essential part of the Sud Est TGV train plan.

Because the PSE alignment brought the new railway into the east side of the Lyon Conurbation, joining the classic network at Sathonay, a series of works was necessary involving the whole of the Lyon area, the highlight of which is the excellent new station at Lyon Part-Dieu. Lyon Part-Dieu is the hub of the SNCF network with interchange between TGVs, classic long-distance trains, and local TER regional services. Lyon Perrache – the former main station – has been retained, but as the layout is constrained by short platforms and a long tunnel at the north end it was quite unsuitable for the level of new traffic generated by TGV.

While the extensive programme of new works, including strategically placed grade-separated junctions, was initiated to segregate traffic flows and eliminate potential conflictions, traffic density in the Lyon area is an on-going problem. The opening of the first stage of the Rhône Alpes line in December 1992 – when Paris-Grenoble TGVs which previously coupled/uncoupled with Lyon units in Part-Dieu station were transferred to the new direct route – provided some relief. Even so, traffic continues to increase. With the completion of the Rhône Alpes line in June 1995, all TGVs – around 12 in each direction – between Paris and the Rhône Valley, Montpellier, Marseille and Nice were transferred to the new route, but they have now been replaced by an additional seven Jonction TGVs from Lille and Brussels, some of which terminate at Lyon and with others going through to the South rejoining the Rhône Alpes line at Grenay.

The core of the PSE train working plan is the 528 kilometres (328 miles) of 270/300 km/h double-track, reversibly-signalled route from Créteil/Lieusaint to St-Marcel-les-Valence, where all trains can be timed at equal speeds within the current headway of five minutes. On the face of things, allocating paths over the 528-kilometre core should be fairly straightforward, but the challenge for SNCF's timetable specialists arises at the five interface points with the classic network – Aisy for Dijon, Franche Compté and Switzerland; Pont-de-Veyle for Geneva and the Culoz route to the Alpes; Sathonay for the Lyon area; St-Quentin-Fallivier for Chambéry and Grenoble and St-Marcel-lès-Valence for the Rhône Valley line to the South.

Although the high-speed core makes the greater contribution to journey-time, to reach the remoter parts of the Sud Est network TGVs spend some time travelling over secondary – albeit important – routes. France-Suisse TGVs traverse long-sections of low-speed single-track through the Jura mountains between Dôle and Vallorbe, although few other trains use this route. Another single-track route is the 39-kilometre branch from Aix-les-Bains to the important Haute Savoie resort town at Annecy. The 44-kilometre (27-mile) single-track line from St-André-le-Gaz to Chambéry is now the prime TGV route to the Alpes. Instead of leaving the high-speed line at Bifurcation Savoie and following the classic route through Bourg-en-Bresse and Culoz, TGVs from Paris to Chambéry and most of the trains to Annecy now leave the high-speed line at Grenay from where they use the Lyon-Grenoble line as far as St-André-le-Gaz where they join the single-line branch to Chambéry. Although it is a longer – and despite the restricted branch line speeds – it is around 20 minutes quicker from Paris to Chambéry than the previous route through Culoz. Line speeds between Ambérieu and Culoz are restricted by gradients and track geometry;

The main maintenance workshop. *Regis Chessum*

the line has to be shared with a significant flow of international freight traffic up to the border station at Modane. Some seven TGVs in each direction – including the new international service between Paris and Milan – use the St-André-le-Gaz route.

Since 1981 business on Paris Sud Est has grown to the extent that the original fleet of 109 first-generation trainsets built for the line can no longer cover the number of trains in the timetable. Pending delivery of Réseau sets, some Atlantique sets were for a time used to supplement the PSE fleet. As Atlantique sets cannot be serviced at EIMM PSE at Villeneuve-St-Georges – they are too long for the depot and its associated equipment – every second day they had to make the circuitous and time-consuming journey back to Châtillon Depot for regular maintenance. Apart from peak ski days – when some 10 or so Atlantique sets are sent over for Saturday and Sunday duties during January to March – Atlantique sets do not now work on PSE, except for those cross-country services from the west and south west of France to Lyon.

At the time of writing in 1997, the PSE fleet – which now comprises various types of PSE trains, two types of Réseau trains and a small number of Duplex trains now coming off the production line from GEC Alsthom – is passing through a transitionary phase. From the outset it was necessary to have three PSE passenger versions – two-class two-voltage; two-class three-voltage; and first-class two-voltage. Given the decision to install TVM 430 on the southern section of the Rhône Alpes line, some 65 two-class two-voltage sets have been equipped with this system. Separate rosters have to be prepared for two-voltage sets according to the type of cab-signalling equipment.

As the PSE renovation programme proceeds, a number of two-class two-voltage sets have been uprated for 300 km/h and equipped with TVM 430 and changed seating layouts. Because these have fewer seats than the original PSE sets, a further set of separate rosters is necessary so that the type of train provided for a specific service conforms with the seat reservation system. Separate rosters were also needed for the two-class three-voltage sets and for the first-class two-voltage sets, although these are now withdrawn for conversion.

The influx of 17 Réseau sets to increase Paris Sud Est capacity was welcome, but once again there are two different versions – 11 two-class two-current and six two-class three-current for working into Italy. These six three-current versions have a different pantograph suitable for Italian current collection and cab-signalling. Separate rosters are necessary for these two Réseau versions. The final version in the PSE fleet is the Duplex; as these trains are quite different from any other train on the route separate rosters are again necessary.

Having agreed the number of trainsets that can be made available for service at particular times, the next task is to weave the work of these units into the fabric of the timetable plan. Reconciling the desire to maximise the use of trains against the discipline imposed by the needs of the maintenance cycle is a difficult task. The nature of the PSE service is such that all trains either depart from or return to Paris at least once per day; some trains make two or more return trips into/out of Paris. Rosters must allow for the maintenance work cycle to be met at the specified time or accumulation of kilometres. Deployment of individual trainsets is by means of a system of work 'days' through which trainsets cycle; the cycle provides time for visits to Bercy Conflans for various levels of short-term maintenance. The cycles do not allow for extended visits for major maintenance. As well as the need to meet the constraints of the maintenance cycle, there is also the issue of trainset positioning. Matching arrivals with return services is not a problem on high-frequency routes such as Paris to Lyon, but as demand for TGV services to more remote or distant parts of the national network has increased, positioning is critical. A case in point is Paris-Nice. Outside the summer peak there are two daily services in each direction, the times of which are chosen to suit the needs of a prime target market: the leisure traveller. Departures from Paris are at 1112 and 1354, arriving in Nice at 1738 and 2022; departures from Nice are at 0952 and 1256, arriving in Paris at 1624 and 1922. As there is no scope to use these trains overnight, both have to stand at Nice until the following morning.

Whilst the 2-hour Paris Gare-de-Lyon – Lyon Part-Dieu schedule is the benchmark for Sud Est timetable production, there are now a number of interesting variations. From summer 1996, almost all trains from Paris to the Sud Est have been routed by the new line from Créteil through Coubert rejoining the original route at Crisenoy. Although this is around 3 kilometres longer than the original route, the line speed is 270 km/h whereas a much lower speed applies over the old route until the start of the PSE line at Lieusaint. Theoretical running times via the Jonction Ouest are a few minutes less than the old route, but for the present this gain is being used to offset the additional time now inserted into PSE schedules necessary because of temporary speed restrictions imposed between St-Florentin and Mâcon until the track renewal programme now in progress is complete. This is likely to continue until 2000 when TGV Méditerranée is commissioned.

Another factor is superior traction performance. Réseau and Duplex trainsets, now used for a number of PSE services, have a much higher power-to-power weight ratio than the older PSE sets. They have better acceleration and greater ability to cope with the steeper gradients on the PSE line. When the renovation of the southern section of the line is complete, and when sufficient PSE sets have been uprated, SNCF hopes to raise the line speed to 300 km/h and introduce a 1 hour 50 minute schedule between Paris and Lyon.

The table opposite details 14 particularly interesting PSE journeys ranked by speed. Fastest daily journey currently is TGV 907 (1436 Paris to Grenoble) which runs non-stop to Satolas in 1 hour 55 minutes – a *vitesse commerciale* of 230 km/h (143.3 mph). Seven journeys have average speeds exceeding 200 km/h (125 mph).

Additional platforms have been built at the Paris Gare-de-Lyon terminal station to cope with new traffic generated by TGV and other services. Brian Perren

Very long non-stop journeys are an important timetable feature. These are made possible by train crew working arrangements. Staff work to a point up to the maximum permitted hours within a shift of duty where they sign off and rest in one of the hostels provided by the SNCF at strategic points throughout the network. Because of the size of the SNCF network, French drivers have a far more extensive route knowledge than their contemporaries on other European railways. Drivers are required to sign that they have knowledge – location of stations, points, signals, gradients, other specific features etc – of the routes required to work. The longest regular non-stop journey – currently in Europe and probably in the world – is between Paris and Marseille – a distance of 783 kilometres (486.6 miles). A pair of Paris-Nice TGVs are publicly advertised as non-stop trains between Paris and St-Raphaël on the Mediterranean Coast, but there is a short comfort stop for the driver at Valence.

Traffic supervision is managed from the Paris Sud Est PAR located near the Gare-de-Lyon; the Rhône Alpes line is controlled from a separate PAR in Lyon.

Paris Sud Est: Operating Highlights

Journey Sector	Distance		Time		Average Speed		
	Km	Miles	Hr	Min	Km/h	Mph	Notes
Paris Satolas TGV	442	274.7	1	55	230.6	143.3	
Paris–Valence	538	334.3	2	24	224.2	139.3	
Paris–Mâcon Loché	366	227.4	1	38	224.1	139.3	
Paris–Le Creusot	306	190.1	1	23	221.2	137.5	
Paris–Lyon Part-Dieu	430	267.2	2	00	215.0	133.6	[1]
Paris–Bourg-en-Bresse	406	252.3	1	59	204.7	127.2	
Paris–Avignon	662	411.4	3	16	202.7	126.0	
Paris–Grenoble	558	346.7	2	57	189.2	117.6	
Paris–Marseille	783	486.6	4	12	186.4	115.8	[4]
Paris–Chambéry	532	330.6	2	58	179.3	111.4	[2]
Paris–Dijon	287	178.3	1	40	172.2	107.0	
Lyon–Valence	118	73.3	0	42	168.6	104.8	
Paris–St-Raphaël	941	584.7	5	37	167.5	104.1	[3]
Bellegarde–Paris	520	323.1	3	08	166.0	103.1	

[1] Paris Sud Est flagship service
[2] Via Lyon Satolas and St-André-le-Gaz
[3] Advertised non-stop, but schedule includes 3-minute driver comfort stop at Valence
[4] Longest non-stop journey in Europe

Formed with two Duplex sets – offering 1,032 seats – the 1400 from Paris to Lyon heads out of the Gare-de-Lyon. *Brian Perren*

Atlantique

While the same basic principles apply, the characteristics of the Atlantique service are quite different from Paris Sud Est. There is no core traffic flow equal in volume or intensity to that between Paris and Lyon; the populations of the largest centres on the network are relatively small. As the network serves a number of holiday resorts, the market tends to be influenced by leisure rather than business travel.

While the route kilometreage is less than the PSE, the high-speed tracks start only 5 km from Paris Montparnasse station and – with a maximum speed of 300 rather than 270 km/h – some very fast journey times are achieved, but over shorter distances. Another interesting operating feature is the upgrading of sections of classic route so that TGVs continue to run at quite high speeds, up to 220 km/h (136.7 mph), to reach their final destination.

Point-to-point running times for the Atlantique line produce some very fast journey times. On the South Western (Aquitaine) branch typical running time for the 231.5 km from Paris Montparnasse to the end of the South Western branch at Monts Junction is 56 minutes – an average speed of 248.0 km/h (154.1 mph). The time from Paris Montparnasse to the end of Brittany branch (km 179.6) is 46 minutes – an average speed of 234.3 km/h (145.6 mph).

Consisting of only 278 route-kilometres which is covered in around 1 hour, trains on the Atlantique spend a greater proportion of their time running on classic tracks cohabiting with regional stopping services and to a lesser extent slower-moving freight trains. All trains using the line – Atlantique sets and Réseau sets from Lille – have the potential to run at the full 300 km/h line speed. Train paths are based on equal speed. With the completion of the Jonction line described elsewhere, there is a now a total of 10 trains in each direction which join the route at Massy TGV station. The key section of the route – used by some 65 basic services in each direction increased in number on peak days – is the 117 kilometres (72.5 miles) between Massy and Courtalain, the junction for the Brittany and Aquitaine branches.

Consequently, traffic densities on the branches – 36 trains each way towards Le Mans and 29 trains each way towards Tours – are lower than other TGV routes. Vendôme, the only other station on the line, is located on the Aquitaine branch, but as only four trains each way call there, the impact on pathing is negligible.

Connections between TGVs and local services play an important part in marketing through journeys from local stations, in particular to and from Paris. The main connectional centres are Rennes, Nantes and Tours. From its complicated series of flat junctions, dead-end terminal station and level of freight activity at St-Pierre-de-Corps, pathing trains in the Tours area can pose problems. Another factor is the pathing of trains between Monts Junction and Bordeaux St-Jean station. While upgrading has enabled TGVs to travel from Monts to Bordeaux in around 2 hours (average speed 109 mph), the need to operate with two block sections reduces line capacity. Fitting in local services can therefore be difficult.

A major feature of the Atlantique project was the complete remodelling of Paris Montparnasse track layout and passenger facilities and construction of the combined TGV trainset servicing depot and maintenance centre at Châtillon. Unlike the other two Paris EIMM TGV centres – Villeneuve-St-Georges and Le Landy – Châtillon is equipped to deal with the longer 20-vehicle (10 articulated passenger coaches plus two power cars) rakes.

All Atlantique TGV operations – train movements, power supplies, maintenance arrangements and trainset disposal – are supervised from the *Poste d'Aiguillage et de la Regulation* (PAR) located at Montparnasse, adjacent to the station signalling centre. The PAR interfaces with the station signalling centre from Montparnasse and fringe signal boxes at Le Mans and Tours where the Atlantique line plugs into the classic network.

Originally intended for the Brittany and Aquitaine TGV routes, the 105 Atlantique trainsets are now also used for cross-country journeys from the west and south west of France to Lyon and Lille. To cover workings from Bordeaux, Nantes and Rennes over TGV Nord Europe to Lille, 20 Atlantique sets have been equipped with TVM 430. These work out from Châtillon on a normal service from Montparnasse to Bordeaux from where they make a return trip to Lille before returning to Paris for their periodic routine maintenance.

Given the importance of the leisure market, the maximum deployment of trainsets is from Friday through to Monday when 92 units are in service on a typical day during the winter peak season. On Tuesday to Thursday the demand is lower, with 78 sets in service covering 99,551 kilometres; this off-peak period enables the engineers to concentrate maintenance during these days.

Atlantique: Operating Highlights

Journey Sector	Distance		Time		Average Speed	
	Km	Miles	Hr	Min	Km/h	Mph
Massy TGV–St-Pierre-des-Corps	206.9	128.6	0	51	243.4	151.2
Paris Montparnasse–Vendôme	161.6	100.4	0	40	242.4	150.6
Paris Montparnasse–St-Pierre-des-Corps	220.8	137.2	0	56	236.6	147.0
Paris Montparnasse–Le Mans	201.6	125.3	0	54	224.0	139.2
Paris Montparnasse–Poitiers	320.9	199.4	1	27	221.3	137.5
Paris Montparnasse–Bordeaux	568.3	353.1	2	54	196.0	121.8
Paris Montparnasse–Nantes	385.7	239.7	1	59	194.5	120.9
Paris Montparnasse–Rennes	363.8	226.1	2	02	178.9	111.2

Nord Europe and Jonction

Three quite distinct types of traffic form the Nord Europe and Jonction traffic base – domestic services between Paris and the Nord Pas-de-Calais region with relatively short journey times; long-distance domestic Jonction TGVs to the south east, west and south west of France; and the increasing number of international services to London and other UK destinations and to Brussels, Köln (Cologne) and Amsterdam. When Eurostar and THALYS services reach their full business potential the number of trains over the critical 135-kilometre (83-mile) core section of the route between Vémars (where the Jonction line diverges) and Croisilles (the junction for Arras) could be as high as 80 trains in each direction, with more on peak days. Although each of the four train service groups is a separate business sector with its own financial bottom line, they all work over common infrastructure. For this reason it is simpler to regard the Nord Europe and Jonction line as a single operating entity.

As was the case with the Sud Est and Atlantique lines, a major programme of works was implemented to adapt key points in the existing classic network to handle the vast increase in the number of train movements necessary to cope with the new levels of business. The major item was the complete remodelling of the Paris Gare du Nord terminal station area and the 16 kilometres (10 miles) of multi-track infrastructure from there out to the start of the new line at Gonesse. Although changes were also necessary in the Lille area – in particular at Lille Flandres station and at Fives stabling sidings – these were on a smaller scale. Most of the additional traffic at Lille is handled at the new Lille Europe station.

The Gare du Nord is one of the busiest stations in Europe. Prior to the launch of the first Nord Europe TGV service to Lille in May 1993, Paris Nord was handling around 2,100 train movements and 500,000 passengers a day. In the longer term this could rise to around 700,000 passengers a day. This traffic comprises international passengers from Britain, Belgium, the Netherlands, Germany, Scandinavia, and even as far as Moscow; longer-distance commuters from the Ile de France and Picardie Regions (the Grande Couronne); and shorter-distance passengers from the busy inner-suburban areas out as far as Creil and stations on RER Line B. Increasing numbers of people with jobs in Paris are now moving to new housing developments in the Grande Couronne. Medium-distance travel into Paris from towns such as Amiens and St Quentin is also growing. Another factor is new business on suburban and RER services by passengers travelling to Paris Nord to join TGVs.

A major reorganisation of the Gare du Nord approach tracks, depot facilities and passenger amenities was necessary to cope with new traffic generated by domestic TGVs, Eurostar and THALYS international high speed services, plus the growth of commuter business. This picture shows the refurbished concourse.
Brian Perren

Three-voltage Réseau set in SNCF livery draws into Brussels Midi station with a service from Paris Nord.
Regis Chessum

During the next few years TGV services are expected to increase to some 70 trains a day into and out of the station – 18 each way for Lille and Tourcoing, 10 a day to Dunkerque/ Valenciennes, one to Cambrai, three to Calais/Boulogne, 20 Eurostars to London, Edinburgh and Manchester and 18 to Brussels, many of which will go on to Cologne (Köln) or Amsterdam. With 70 TGVs arriving and departing each day, the present 4.4 million domestic traffic base is expected to rise to 8.65 million; this figure includes traffic to Lille which is expected to double reaching 5.25 million. International expectations are 16.5 million for Eurostar to Britain and 6.25 for Brussels and beyond. There were just 11 million passengers a year using these services in 1985; by 2000 there will be around 30 million – a threefold increase.

The purpose of the Gare du Nord reorganisation was to adapt the approach tracks, platforms, servicing facilities and maintenance depots to provide more capacity needed for the changeover to TGV-style operations. Passenger amenities – circulating areas, ticket sales points, buffets, waiting areas, shops etc – have been enlarged and enhanced. Under the old regime, the station was divided into arrival and departure sections with separate approach and departure tracks. Almost all long-distance trains were taken out to the old Landy sidings to be serviced for their return trip and then brought back into the departure side of the station. TGVs will mostly turnround in the station platforms. Also, a new TGV maintenance facility was necessary, located close to the terminus. These factors – plus the changes to connect TGV Nord Europe tracks at Gonesse – determined the redesign.

In the new station the number of platforms has been reduced from 33 to 32. There are 19 tracks in the new main line station, although Nos. 1 (122 metres) and 2 (205 metres) are for standing locomotives or vans. All of the 17 tracks – 3 to 19 – have been lengthened well beyond the old throat. Of the 17 tracks, 14 are 405 metres long and Nos 15, 16 and 17 are 329 metres. A total of 17 platforms can now accommodate a Eurostar (394 metres) or two Réseau, PBKA or Duplex units coupled in multiple measuring 400.4 metres. To enable security checks to be undertaken on Eurostar trains departing for Britain, platforms 3, 4, 5 and 6 have been secured and fenced off; access to the 'Gare de Londres' is strictly supervised. The modified suburban surface station now consists of nine platforms numbered 20 and 21 and 30 to 36 (numbering is not consecutive); 20 and 21 are refuges for emergency use. Under the new regime, the main line platforms are now relieved of all suburban trains. Although the platforms have not been modified, the RER sub-surface platforms should be included to complete the picture. These are numbered 41, 43, 44 and 42.

Previously, the extensive facilities at Le Landy (also on the west side of the layout) were for maintenance and servicing of locomotive-hauled main-line stock. Heavy maintenance was also undertaken at Le Landy; the double-deck TGV mock-ups were built there. The site has been transformed. The complex is now in three parts:

Three TGV types – Eurostar, Réseau and PBKA – are serviced at Le Landy Sud. Note the smaller Eurostar profile compared with the two Réseau sets. *Regis Chessum*

Le Landy Sud (south): This is for TGV trainset servicing – internal and external cleaning, watering, toilet flushing, and safety checks with running gear and pantographs. There are six inspection tracks, four for short turnrounds and three for stabling.

Le Landy Centre: As rebuilding the old carriage depot and workshops for TGVs was not feasible, all buildings and tracks on this 35,000 square metre site were cleared to make way for three new buildings. Eurostar maintenance is undertaken in the 420-metre facility. Other TGV trainset maintenance – replacement of major components, bogies and transformers etc – is undertaken in a second four-track building. Maintenance work for PBKA and international trainsets is undertaken in the third building.

Le Landy Pleyel: This area has been designed for locomotive-hauled stock and for double-deck (suburban and outer-suburban trainsets), although capable of dealing with TGVs if necessary. Sidings have been extended out to handle 400-metre trains and there is ample space for shunting-out individual coaches from locomotive-hauled trainsets. The entire Le Landy site is controlled from a centre (OCTGV) at Le Landy Sud.

Passenger amenities have been comprehensively remodelled. This too has been a demanding challenge for the architects and engineers – for access to the station is severely constrained by the local road network and the location of the two Métro lines serving it. There are three passenger levels in the new station – sub-surface, street-level and an upper-level. The sub-surface level has been developed from the existing access to the Métro and RER on the east side of the station; escalators or stairways give access to the ground (ie platform) level. A large 35,000 square metre five-level sub-surface car park capable of holding 1,300 vehicles has been dug out and built at the west 'Gare de Londres' end of the station. Taxi flow has been reorganised so that departing passengers are taken to a new sub-surface entrance; arriving passengers use a new sub-surface taxi rank on the west side of the station. There is a commercial area with buffets and shops at this level. Most passengers will circulate at ground level where the information and ticket sales points are located. The old upper level offices have been removed to make space for a second commercial area for shops and cafes, additional ticket selling points and the security area for passengers boarding Eurostar trains to Britain.

On a typical day the Gare du Nord handles 667 arrivals and departures – a total of 1,334 train movements. In the morning 0700–0900 peak period, a total of 133 trains arrive – a train every 54 seconds. Similarly, there are 135 departures between 1700 and 1900 in the evening peak. In the two peak periods there is an RER train every 2 full minutes.

Although as discussed in Chapter 4, the Nord Europe line runs through the centre of the city of Lille which has a dedicated TGV station at Lille Europe, there is extensive interaction between the high-speed line and the existing classic network. The original dead-end terminal station – now upgraded and renamed Lille Flandres – remains the terminal for TGVs to and from Paris Nord. Access to Lille Flandres is by a bi-directional single-track chord some three kilometres from the station. To provide the temporary route from Lille Europe to Brussels Midi for Eurostar trains pending the opening of the Belgian high-speed line from Wannehain, another single-track chord was put in at the Paris end of Lille Europe station providing access to the hitherto little-used line to the Belgian border at Baisieux. This also entailed 11 kilometres (6.8 miles) of 25 kV electrification on the French side of the frontier and further 3 kV dc electrification from Baisieux to Tournai. There is a third single-track chord on the Calais side of Lille Europe at Hondeghem (PRCI 44). For a few months before Lille Europe station was commissioned, this connection was used by a daily Paris – Calais Ville TGV, but this is now only used in emergencies. As Lille is the starting point for a range of TGV services, facilities for the stabling, cleaning and light maintenance of TGV trainsets had to be provided at Fives. These are located at the Paris end of the Lille railway complex, with access both from Lille Europe and Lille Flandres.

With the opening of TGV Nord Europe together with the continuing expansion of the TER regional passenger network, the Lille area – which also handles a significant volume of short and long-distance freight traffic – is now a very busy railway centre. There are a number of potential constraints – including the fact that all TGVs going forward to Tourcoing have to reverse in Lille Flandres station before continuing their journey – which determines the structure of the timetable.

So far as the Calais area is concerned, most TGV activity is of Eurostars heading for or coming out of the Channel Tunnel, although a number of these call at Calais Fréthun TGV station. The main changes in the Calais area were for Channel Tunnel freight, involving the construction of new marshalling yards and exchange facilities, but this work also enabled electrically-hauled trains to run to Calais Ville. However, as part of the general upgrading of rail infrastructure in the area, SNCF electrified 40 kilometres of route from Calais Les Fontinettes to Boulogne Ville. This electrification was commissioned in October 1993. There is a direct daily service in each direction between Paris and Boulogne via Lille Europe and Calais Fréthun where the train has to reverse direction.

Train supervision, operation of points, control of power supplies and day-to-day operational disposal of trainsets for the Nord Europe line is managed from the *Poste d'Aiguillage et de la Regulations* (PAR) located at Lille. The Lille PAR adjoins the international control centre which regulates the Eurostar service including liaison with SNCB, Eurotunnel, Railtrack in the UK and Eurostar UK.

With the exception of some Atlantique trainsets used on Lille-Europe–Bordeaux Jonction trains and the odd uprated PSE set used on winter weekend ski trains, the Nord Europe-Jonction timetable is covered exclusively by two or three-voltage Réseau sets based at Le Landy. Although also based at Le Landy, Eurostar, PBA and PBKA trainsets – which also travel over TGV Nord Europe – are regarded as separate international fleets. However, from time-to-time, in emergency circumstances, it is not unknown for one of these international trainsets to be pressed into service to cover a domestic working.

As their name implies – Réseau is French for network – these trains are the most versatile TGVs in the SNCF fleet. They can go practically anywhere; some are equipped with 3 kV dc for working into Belgium (and Italy) to cover the increasing range of Jonction services from Brussels to points in France, including a Brussels–Nice service, the longest such TGV journey.

On a typical winter mid-week day a total of 38 two-voltage sets would be in service. Total kilometres covered is 43,408, an average of 1,142 kilometres per unit; some units are reserved to cover contingencies. As the cross-country Jonction service is a Lille-based operation, but as the sets are based at Le Landy (Paris) for maintenance, the daily rosters include some positioning trips to get trains to or back from Le Landy depot. Some of these journeys operate as passenger trains, but some empty stock working is necessary, although these positioning journeys only take one hour. On this programme the overnight fleet dispersal is at 16 different locations throughout France with one unit actually in service at night. There is a number of two-unit workings – Lille Europe to Avignon with separate units for Marseille and Montpellier, and Lille Europe to Le Mans with separate units for Nantes and Rennes. The daily service between Rouen and Lyon Perrache via Versailles and Massy Palaiseau is incorporated with a working from Lille Europe to Lyon Perrache.

Because they are required to work into Belgium, separate programmes are required for the Landy-based fleet of three-voltage Réseau units. Daily requirements are 19 units for mid-week and 22 units for the four days from Friday through to Monday. These also include work for the 10 PBA units to cover the four daily return THALYS services between Paris Nord and Amsterdam Central. Only PBA units can work through to Amsterdam, but the normal SNCF three-voltage Réseau units can work to any point in Belgium. The Amsterdam rosters are grouped in cycles so that the PBA units are always available for this service between visits to Le Landy for routine maintenance. The overnight stabling demonstrates the operating range and versatility of these units. Long journeys – 1326 kilometres (824 miles) from Brussels Midi to Nice for example – are a feature of their utilisation. Another interesting working involves two units covering TGV 9526 departing at 0701 from Brussels Midi to Marseille arriving at 1445; this unit returns at 1554 to Brussels. On the southbound journey, a second unit is attached at Lille Europe and for Montpellier which is detached at Avignon; both units return as a two-unit formation Montpellier to Lille Europe and Marseille to Brussels Midi. The return distance between Brussels Midi and Marseille is 2241 kilometres (1393 miles). Another unit covers a return service from Brussels Midi to Bordeaux – a round trip of 1940 kilometres (1206 miles).

Nord Europe and Jonction: Operating Highlights

Journey Sector	Distance		Time		Average Speed	
	Km	Miles	Hr	Min	Km/h	Mph
Paris Nord–Lille Flandres	226	140.4	1	01	222.3	138.1
Paris Nord–Arras	179	111.2	0	49	219.2	136.2
Paris Nord–Calais Fréthun	327	203.2	1	23	236.4	146.9
Charles-de-Gaulle TGV– Lille Europe	202	125.5	0	49	247.3	153.7
Charles-de-Gaulle TGV– Satolas TGV	454	282.1	1	56	234.8	145.9
Marne-le-Vallée–Lyon Part Dieu	418	259.8	1	53	221.9	137.9
Calais Fréthun–Lille Europe	101	62.7	0	29	209.0	129.9

MASTER PLAN REVISED

In January 1989 the French Government prepared a master plan for the development of high-speed rail services. Its purpose was to ensure that future infrastructure investment would take account of both national and regional factors and would establish cohesion between different transport modes. Following extensive discussions between the government, the French Regions and SNCF, the Master Plan was approved by the government in April 1992. Although this gave the Master Plan full status under French planning procedures, it was not a definitive programme *per se,* but a list of desirable options to be developed as part of an on-going strategy. Each TGV project has to pass through seven planning stages leading to the *Déclaration d'Utilité Publique* (DUP).

Comprising 16 projects for new or upgraded routes, the Master Plan envisaged a network of around 4,700 kilometres, of which 700 kilometres were already in service and another 560 kilometres were under construction. The cost of the plan at 1989 values was 210 billion Francs – 180 billion for infrastructure and 30 billion for rolling stock. As well as new radial routes from Paris to the Regions, the plan also included a number of important new cross-country links. Given France's position in the centre of Europe, a number of projects were also essential items in the emerging European high-speed rail plan.

Given the success of the Paris Sud Est line – which generated a 15% internal SNCF rate of return, a 30% socio-economic benefit and amortisation of capital in 10 years – the prognosis for high-speed rail at the start of the 1990s seemed to be very good. Completed in 1989, the Atlantique project also showed a positive 12% internal SNCF rate of return and a 23% socio-economic benefit.

To some extent the success of the Paris Sud Est and Atlantique routes was achieved on the back of very favourable economic conditions, but by the start of the 1990s these began to change. As well as being hit by the severity of the economic recession which affected both leisure and business travel, competition from the deregulated internal French air services together with expansion of the national autoroute network was taking traffic from key TGV routes such as Paris – Bordeaux and Paris – Geneva, both of which generated significant first class revenue. By the time the Nord Europe and Rhône Alpes projects opened for traffic, the business on offer did not achieve the economic forecast which had been used to make the financial case for this investment.

Whilst the recession could be regarded as a cyclic change which would be followed by more prosperous circumstances, a most significant development was the cost of constructing new 'greenfields' TGV projects. As TGV routes increased in number it was inevitable they would have to pass through – or close to – areas of environmental sensitivity. The passage of TGV Méditerranée through Provence is a particular case in point. Whereas the cost per kilometre for the Atlantique line was about FFR 35 million, it was FFR 40 million for TGV Nord Europe and a staggering FFR 65 million for the Méditerranée project. Given such levels of costs, only a few of the original Master Plan proposals were now viable.

At the same time as SNCF's financial crisis was gaining momentum, the TGV Est Éuropéen project was making its formal progress through the DUP procedures. Government approval was announced on 14 May 1996. So far as the choice of route alignment and other technical details were concerned, this was good news for SNCF, but since the long enquiry process had started the loss of traffic, particularly from the Strasbourg

LES LIGNES A GRANDE VITESSE
THE HIGH - SPEED LINES

En service en TGV network by 1996	Extensions prochaines Forthcoming extensions	A l'étude Under study	Total en France Total length in France
1280 KM	**640 KM**	**1400 KM**	**3320 KM**

MER DU NORD
NORTH SEA

London

Amsterdam
Rotterdam
Antwerpen
Bruxelles

Calais Dunkerque
Lille-Europe
Lille Flandres Liège
Boulogne
Arras

Tunnel sous la Manche
Channel tunnel
1994

MANCHE
ENGLISH CHANNEL

Valenciennes
Cambrai Charleville Luxembourg
TGV NORD
1993
TGV Haute
Picardie
Saarbrücken
TGV EST
2000/2001

Rouen
Aéroport
CDG TGV
Reims
Metz
München

Frankfurt

TGV ATLANTIQUE
1989/1990
PARIS
Massy Marne la Vallée Bar-le-Duc
Nancy St-Dié Strasbourg
JONCTION EST
1994/1996
Épinal

Brest
St Brieuc
TGV BRETAGNE
Colmar
Mulhouse
TGV RHIN-RHÔNE
Remiremont

Quimper
Rennes Le Mans
Basel

Lorient Vannes
Vendôme
Dijon Belfort
Besançon
Bern
Zürich

Le Croisic
La Baule St Nazaire
Angers Tours
TGV SUD-EST
1981/1983
Le Creusot TGV
Chalon
Lausanne
Brig

Nantes
TGV
PAYS DE LA LOIRE
Niort Poitiers
Mâcon TGV
Genève

La Rochelle
TGV AQUITAINE
Lyon Satolas
TGV Annecy
Chambéry
TGV
LYON-TURIN
Milano

OCÉAN ATLANTIQUE
ATLANTIC OCEAN
Angoulême
St-Étienne
Grenoble Modane
Torino

Bordeaux
Valence
TGV RHÔNE-ALPES
1992/1994

Agen
TGV MÉDITERRANÉE
1999/2000
Nîmes
Avignon
Nice Ventimiglia

Arcachon
Montauban
Montpellier
Marseille

Bayonne
Hendaye
Dax
Toulouse
Pau Tarbes Carcassonne Béziers
Toulon

Lourdes
Narbonne
TGV SUD
MONTPELLIER - BARCELONE
Perpignan

MÉDITERRANÉE
MEDITERRANEAN SEA

Legend:

— Ligne nouvelle en service
  Existing high-speed line

— Extensions prochaines
  Forthcoming extensions

— Phase ultérieure
  Subsequent phase

••• Projets à l'étude
  Projects under study

—•— Ligne classique empruntée par les TGV
  Conventional line used by high-speed trains

◉ Gare nouvelle
  New station

SNCF
GRANDES LIGNES
Département Développement

area, had undermined the original business case on which the project was based. At best, SNCF's 4.3% internal rate of return was not a ringing endorsement for the project; these changed circumstances suggested that the internal rate might be as low as 1%. Concerned by this turn of events the French government asked SNCF for a reappraisal not only of TGV Est Éuropéen but also of the entire Master Plan which it had so readily endorsed in 1992. A former president of SNCF – Philippe Rouvillois – was commissioned to review the Master Plan and recommend a new strategy.

Published in October 1996, the Rouvillois report proposed new general criteria for high-speed infrastructure; these were used to reappraise the 16 Master Plan projects. Henceforth, where new high-speed lines could be justified, construction should be phased so that costs could be spread; tilting train technology should be used to obtain higher speeds where the case for new construction is not viable; to maximise connections between TGVs and other regional services; and new stations in greenfield locations such as Haute Picardie should be avoided. Future new lines should be designed so that they could carry freight traffic at night.

Rouvillois proposed a drastically reduced Master Plan comprising a total of around 3,320 kilometres, of which 1,280 kilometres are already in service. The next extensions, totalling around 640 kilometres, are TGV Méditerranée, the construction of which is now well under way and should be completed in 1999–2000, and TGV Est Éuropéen.

Although the *Déclaration d'Utilité Publique* (DUP) for TGV Est Européen was announced on 14 May 1996 – the core of which is 400 or so kilometres of new railway infrastructure from Vaires-sur-Marne (23 kilometres from Paris Est) to Vendenheim (10 kilometres from Strasbourg) – the French Government waited for the Rouvillois report before deciding its future. On 23 December 1996 it announced that the first stage – 268 kilometres of new railway from Vaires to Vandières in the Moselle Valley – would go ahead. Detailed design has taken place in 1997 with construction starting in 1998. (TGV Est Européen is described later in this book).

Eight 1992 Master Plan projects are retained. They are:

1. Rhine–Rhône Cross-country route, Dijon – Mulhouse 190 kilometres. Links the Alsace and Rhône Alpes regions; important part of the European high-speed network from Switzerland and Germany to Spain. Two stations – Besançon and Belfort – proposed. Potential route for accelerated TGV service from Zürich, Basel and Belfort to Paris via Dijon and Paris Sud Est line. Future role of non-electrified route from Paris Est to Basel would be re-appraised. Cost: infrastructure 12 billion Francs, SNCF contribution 4.8 billion. Trainsets: 12. Proposal at preliminary engineering stage.

2. Lyon–Montmélian: New line – first stage of Lyon – Turin international project – from Lyon (near Satolas Airport) to Montmélian near Chambéry: 85 kilometres. European priority project. Joint French-Italy project group established. Feasibility study stage.

3. Montmélian–Turin: Second stage of Lyon – Turin project. Involves two major tunnels – 19 kilometres Belledonne tunnel in France and 54-kilometre tunnel from St-Jean-De-Maurienne to Suse in Italy. Route would be used by freight shuttle trains – rolling highway – as well as passenger trains. Cost of this project, together with the Lyon-Montmélian new line is around 50 billion francs.

4. Sillon–Alpin: Alpine project from Montmélian through the Alpes Savoie to Geneva. Study group formed to investigate proposal.

5. TGV Aquitaine Extension of Atlantique line from Tours to Bordeaux: 301 kilometres. Cost: infrastructure 18.6 billion Francs, SNCF contribution 8.3 billion Francs. Five additional trainsets required.

6.   TGV Bretagne–Pays De Le Loire Extension of western (Brittany) branch of the Atlantique line, from where it currently ends at Connerré, by-passing the town of Le Mans to near the town of Sablé from where there will be separate branches joining existing classic routes at Rennes (for Brest and Quimper), and Angers (for Nantes): 225 kilometres. Cost: infrastructure 11.7 billion Francs, SNCF contribution 4.7 billion Francs. Two extra trainsets required. Project at preliminary discussion stage.

7.   TGV Languedoc–Roussillon. Extension of western branch of TGV Méditerranée from Montpellier through Perpignon to the Spanish frontier where it would interface with the Spanish AVE line from Barcelona, thereby joining the French and Spanish high-speed networks: 215 kilometres. Thus the Rhine – Rhône, Paris Sud Est, Rhône Alpes and Méditerranée projects would combine to provide a through route from Switzerland, Germany and France to Spain. Identified as an EU priority project. Cost between 14.8 and 15.3 billion Francs (SNCF contribution 3.2 billion Francs). Trainsets 12. Preliminary Engineering stage authorised.

A key Rouvillois' recommendation – endorsed by the French government – that SNCF should consider the use of tilting technology to achieve journey-time reductions signifies an important change of direction. SNCF looked at tilting technology – which enables trains to pass through curves at much higher speeds thereby removing the need for major infrastructure investment – in the early 1970s. These issues are more fully explained in Chapter 35.

In accordance with French statutory planning procedures, proposals for new TGV routes – and other major infrastructure projects – are developed through seven stages:

1. **Opening discussions**: Proposals originate from an on-going dialogue between Central Government in Paris, the Département, Regional Councils, local interest groups and SNCF. Projects with an international dimension are developed by ministers at inter-governmental level.

2. **Feasibility study**: When a proposal has been defined, a feasibility study will be made. This will include preliminary traffic forecasts, socio-economic benefits and a broad idea of the route alignment.

3. **Preliminary engineering**: These studies will form the basis of the Government and SNCF evidence to the Public Enquiry.

4. **Public Enquiry**: Full Public Enquiry with the opportunity for all interested parties to present their support or objections to the proposal. This is an essential preliminary to the next stage – the Declaration of Public Utility (DUP). As the DUP gives the state wide powers – including the compulsory purchase of land – this part of the process is very important.

5. **Déclaration d'Utilité Publique (DUP)**: DUP is the official statutory confirmation that the project is in the public interest and can proceed. Normally, once the DUP process has been completed, agreement to start the project follows within a few months. However, the DUP declaration does not cover the funding of the project which is a separate issue.

6. **Detailed design**: Full engineering specification of the route, infrastructure and rolling stock.

7. **Government approval**: This is the official Government approval for SNCF to start the project; this approval implies that all funding issues have been agreed.

TGV MÉDITERRANÉE

Construction of TGV Méditerranée – SNCF's most contentious high-speed rail route – started in September 1995. While previous TGV routes have mostly passed through open country with relatively minor environmental disturbance, physical considerations were such that the only practical route for the Méditerannée line between Valence and Marseille entailed the passage of the narrow Rhône Valley corridor as far as Avignon and thence alongside the Lubéron National Park to reach the outskirts of Marseille. With its ancient monuments, buildings, villages and towns of great historical interest, Provence is an outstanding area of culture and natural beauty. A particular area of sensitivity is the passage of the Lubéron in the Cavaillon area famed for its farming and fruit and vegetable production. Opposition has been widespread and well-organised. Any TGV route through Provence would have been contentious.

Discussion of the TGV Méditerranée project started in January 1989 when the French Government asked SNCF to study the possibility of extending the Paris Sud Est and Rhône Alpes lines to Marseille and Montpellier to provide a continuous high-speed railway from Paris to the Mediterranean. A cross-border link with Spain to reach Barcelona was also part of this study. In July 1990, SNCF submitted a number of alternative route options to the Government, but opposition was such that a special counsellor of state – supported by eight independent experts – was appointed to consider the social and economic need for a new railway. The project was endorsed.

In October 1992, the Government initiated the 'Déclaration d'Utilitié Publique' (DUP) procedures. Normally, once the DUP process has been initiated, agreement to start the project usually follows in a few months. Under the French planning procedures, full preliminary details incorporating recommendations following local and regional consultations are submitted to government before the DUP process is started. In this case consultations involved 106 local communities, five départements and three régions. The enquiry lasted over 30 months and involved over 2,000 public meetings. Unusually, although the enquiry was concluded in December 1992, in view of the opposition the government decided to have a further inter-ministerial conference before giving the go-ahead. Final approval was given in May 1994 and the DUP was signed by the Prime Minister on 2 June 1994. SNCF approval followed in February 1995. The cost of the project is 24.2 billion francs – around £3 billion and approximately the same as the Channel Tunnel Rail Link – to which the government is contributing ten per cent.

TGV Méditerranée starts near St-Marcel-lès-Valence. At present the Rhône Alpes tracks at St-Marcel-lès-Valence are aligned to take TGVs on to the Grenoble–Valence cross-country line to join the classic PLM line just before Valence station from where they continue their journey to the South. The Mediterranean project starts at km 493 (measured from the start of the original PSE line at Lieusaint 29.4 kilometres from the Gare-de-Lyon in Paris) and consists of 217 kilometres of new route to the outskirts of Marseille, a 32-kilometre branch from a point to the west of Avignon to a point to the east of Nîmes where it feeds into the classic line to Montpellier, plus eight kilometres of connecting tracks. Also included is a further 47 kilometres through to Montpellier, the design for which is complete, but construction of this extension will start later. The Montpellier extension is the first part of TGV Languedoc – Roussillon from Montpellier to Perpignan. In October 1995 the French and Spanish governments signed an accord for the joint development of a high-speed cross-border line from Perpignan to Barcelona. The go-ahead is awaited; target date for completion is 2004.

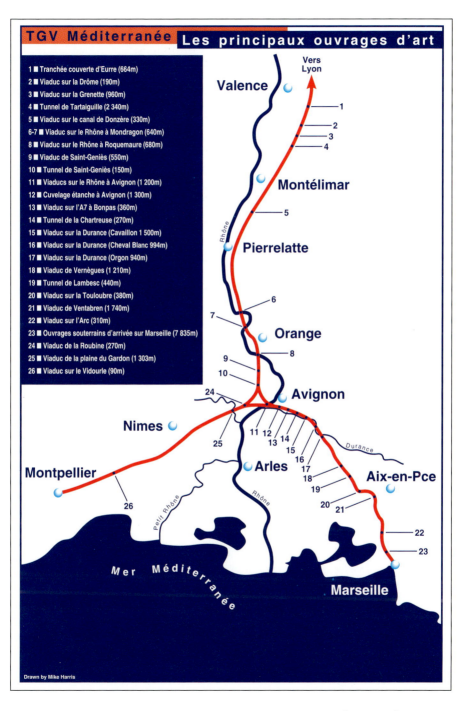

TGV Méditerranée — Les principaux ouvrages d'art

1 ■ Tranchée couverte d'Eurre (664m)
2 ■ Viaduc sur la Drôme (190m)
3 ■ Viaduc sur la Grenette (960m)
4 ■ Tunnel de Tartaiguille (2 340m)
5 ■ Viaduc sur le canal de Donzère (330m)
6-7 ■ Viaduc sur le Rhône à Mondragon (640m)
8 ■ Viaduc sur le Rhône à Roquemaure (680m)
9 ■ Viaduc de Saint-Geniès (550m)
10 ■ Tunnel de Saint-Geniès (150m)
11 ■ Viaducs sur le Rhône à Avignon (1 200m)
12 ■ Cuvelage étanche à Avignon (1 300m)
13 ■ Viaduc sur l'A7 à Bonpas (360m)
14 ■ Tunnel de la Chartreuse (270m)
15 ■ Viaduc sur la Durance (Cavaillon 1 500m)
16 ■ Viaduc sur la Durance (Cheval Blanc 994m)
17 ■ Viaduc sur la Durance (Orgon 940m)
18 ■ Viaduc de Vernègues (1 210m)
19 ■ Tunnel de Lambesc (440m)
20 ■ Viaduc sur la Touloubre (380m)
21 ■ Viaduc de Ventabren (1 740m)
22 ■ Viaduc sur l'Arc (310m)
23 ■ Ouvrages souterrains d'arrivée sur Marseille (7 835m)
24 ■ Viaduc de la Roubine (270m)
25 ■ Viaduc de la plaine du Gardon (1 303m)
26 ■ Viaduc sur le Vidourle (90m)

Vers Lyon

Valence
Montélimar
Pierrelatte
Orange
Avignon
Nimes
Arles
Montpellier
Aix-en-Pce
Marseille

Rhône
Petit Rhône
Rhône
Durance

Mer Méditerranée

Drawn by Mike Harris

For the first 60 or so kilometres from St-Marcel-lès-Valence – which includes the Grenette Viaduct (930 metres) and the Tartaiguille Tunnel (2,400 metres) – the route is well to the east of the River Rhône. At Pierrelatte the line crosses the Donzère Canal, avoiding the nuclear power station at Tricastin, to run parallel with the classic PLM line near Lapalud. Here there will be two emergency single-lead connections with the PLM line – one from St-Marcel-lès-Valence direction Marseille via the PLM and one from Lyon PLM direction towards Marseille via the new TGV line. To get a good alignment south of Lapalud, the railway has to cross and recross the Rhône river on two closely-spaced viaducts – Mondragon Viaduct (640 metres) and Mornas Viaduct (860 metres). Now passing to the east of Orange – one of the famed Provencal historic towns – the line approaches Avignon.

In order to reach the Les Angles area to the west of Avignon, 20 or so kilometres south of Orange the line again crosses to the west side of the River Rhône over the Viaduct de Roquemaure (680 metres). This area is the location for the Les Angles Triangle – a high-speed junction formed by the diverging branches to Nîmes and Marseille and the cross-country link from Nîmes to Marseille which forms the base of the triangle. To permit a speed of 300 km/h the sides of the triangle are five to six kilometres in length and the base is around six kilometres – a total of around 16 kilometres (10 miles) of railway. The distance from the start of the line at St-Marcel-lès-Valence to the northern point of the Les Angles triangle is 122 kilometres (75.7 miles). Given the considerable increase in passenger traffic expected, there will be a new TGV station – Gare du Grand Avignon – to the south of the city. A short rail line to connect the new TGV with the PLM station may be built.

Whereas the classic PLM route from Avignon to Marseille St-Charles follows a longer alignment through Tarascon, Arles and Miramas, from Grand Avignon TGV station the new line heads east. The distance from Grand Avignon to Marseille St-Charles is 94 kilometres via the new line – 27 kilometres less than the PLM line through Arles. For environmental protection the exit from Grand Avignon station is through a 1,300-metre covered section, from where the tracks run alongside the River Durance through Cavaillon to Orgon. Choosing an acceptable route through this part of the Lubéron area – famed for the quality of its fruit and vegetables as well as its historic Provence buildings – posed a number of problems. There is a short 270-metre tunnel at Chartreuse and three viaducts for the railway to cross and recross the River Durance; the longest of these viaducts is 1,500 metres at Cheval Blanc. From Orgon the line runs to the east of the A8 autoroute du soleil and to the west of Aix-en-Provence, but it turns south near Ventabren where there is a 1,740-metre viaduct. Continuing south from Ventabren the line is now on the Plateau D'Arbois where there is to be a major TGV railhead station. Although Arbois station is only 18 or so kilometres from the centre of Marseille, it will serve a wide catchment area formed by a number of communities between the Étang de Berre and Aix-en-Provence.

The nature of the terrain and density of population is such that the final approaches to the centre of Marseille are mostly in tunnel. There are four – Pennes-Mirabeau (1,530 metres), Tranchée Belleperie (400 metres), Marseille Tunnel (5,414 metres) and Tranchée St-Andre (475 metres) – a total of 7,815 metres (4.9 miles). The end of the Valence – Marseille section is at St-André, (270 kilometres from St-Marcel-lès-Valence), where the tracks join the classic PLM line for the final eight kilometres into Marseille St-Charles station. To cope with the extra traffic in the Marseille area, the route from St-André and the layout at St-Charles station will be upgraded and resignalled.

The western Nîmes branch starts at the north side of the Avignon Les Angles triangle joining with the tracks from Grand Avignon station on the west side of the triangle. The alignment is then through open country for 24 kilometres to Redessan, the present end of the project. Here there is a grade junction with the classic line from Tarascon enabling TGVs to run the 11 kilometres to the existing station at Nîmes. Although the remaining 47 kilometres from Redessan to Lunel in the outskirts of Montpellier – which includes a TGV railhead station to the south of Nîmes – has been agreed and designed, construction will not start for the present.

With the exception of some locations in the Avignon area, the line has been designed for a potential speed of 350 km/h (218 mph), but this is very much a long-term aspiration and for the present the maximum speed will be 300 km/h. Space between track centres is 4.8 metres, minimum radius curves are 5,500 metres, and the maximum gradient is 3.5%. Tunnels have been designed to provide 100 sq metres of free air space to allow simultaneous passage of trains at 300 km/h, but the approach tunnels in the Marseille area will be restricted to 230 km/h. Power supplies – from three sub-stations – are 25 kV. The route is signalled for full bi-directional running at 300 km/h; there are 170 km/h crossovers spaced approximately every 25 kilometres. TVM 430 cab-signalling provides 3-minute headways; signalling block sections are 1,500 metres. Signalling, traffic control, security supervision will be undertaken from two centres – St-Marcel-lès-Valence to Lapalud will be managed from Lyon and Lapalud to Marseille will be managed at Marseille.

Although all towns in the region will benefit from the project, highlight journey-time is 3 hours for the 750 kilometres from Marseille to Paris, a *vitesse commerciale* of 250 km/h. This timing assumes a gain of around 10 minutes between Crisenoy and Montanay from the upgrading of the original Paris-Lyon (PSE) line from 270 to 300 km/h. Other times from Marseille include 1 hour 25 minutes to Lyon, 3 hours 35 minutes to Geneva, 3 hours 25 minutes to Roissy Charles-de-Gaulle Airport Paris, 4 hours 20 minutes to Lille and 5 hours 5 minutes to Brussels. With a change to Eurostar at Lille Europe, London can be reached in 7 hours 15 minutes; this will be reduced to around 6 hours 35 minutes with the opening of the Channel Tunnel Rail Link in 2003. Journey times from Avignon are also significantly reduced – 1 hour 5 minutes to Lyon and 2 hours 40 minutes to Paris.

As well as these improvements on the core Marseille/Montpellier – Paris and Marseille – Lyon – Lille route, there will also be a number of interesting regional improvements between towns on the emerging Grand Sud regional network between Marseille, Avignon and Montpellier. A journey time of 55 minutes from Marseille to Montpellier is in prospect – *vitesse commerciale* 215.8 km/h – a reduction of more than 30 minutes on the present classic journey time. Three types of TGV equipment will be used – Duplex, Réseau and refurbished PSE sets. With a 3-hour journey time between Paris and Marseille SNCF is looking to gain a significant share of the Marseille – Paris business market from air as well as generating new journey opportunities to the leisure resorts in this part of France.

TGV MÉDITERRANÉE RAILHEAD STATIONS

Rhône Alpes Sud: Located at St-Marcel-lès-Valence, the new station provides an interchange between the TGV tracks and the classic Grenoble – Valence line, the platforms for which are on an overbridge carrying the classic tracks over the TGV line. The TGV part of the station has two through tracks and two platform loops for stopping services.

Grand Avignon: Avignon is an important railhead. With the launch of TGV Méditerranée and the introduction of significantly reduced journey times between Avignon and Marseille, Toulon and the Côte d'Azur, the number of TGV passengers using the new Grand Avignon station is expected to increase to around 4,000 per day rising to an annual total of between 1.8 and 2.5 million passengers per year.

Arbois: Passengers from the greater Marseille Metropolitan area will have the choice of two TGV stations – the existing terminus at Marseille St-Charles and a new TGV railhead at Arbois. Located between the communes at Aix-en-Provence and Vitrolles on the Étang de Berre, Arbois is expected to generate significant new traffic particularly for business travellers to Paris who would otherwise be deterred by the need to join a Paris-bound TGV at St-Charles station in the centre of the city. When TGV Méditerranée opens, a total of 60 TGVs – 30 in each direction – will serve St-Charles station and 15 to 20 will also call at Arbois. SNCF expects to handle around 10,000 passengers per day at St-Charles and 2,700 passengers per day at Arbois.

TGV EST ÉUROPÉEN

Although the Déclaration d'Utilité Publique (DUP) for TGV Est Éuropéen – the core of which is 400 or so kilometres of new railway infrastructure from Vaires-Sur-Marne (23 kilometres from Paris Est) to Vendenheim (10 kilometres from Strasbourg) – was announced on 14 May 1996 there has been considerable uncertainty regarding the viability and future of the project. Whereas the economics of recent projects such as the Rhône Alpes and Méditerranée extensions to the PSE line have been favourably influenced by the synergy which follows from extensions of existing high-speed infrastructure, TGV Est Éuropéen is a brand new 'greenfield' project which has to carry the initial cost of construction and is dependent on a significant generation of new business. Traffic forecasts submitted by SNCF for the DUP enquiry process, showed that passengers per year would increase from 8.5 million (7.1 million domestic plus 1.4 million international) to 15.5 million (12.5 million domestic plus 3.0 million international), an 80% increase in business. International journeys represents 20% of the business; France-Germany journeys would increase from 0.8 to 2.0 million and France-Swiss journeys from 0.3 million to 0.7 million per year.

Against the background of the current French recession and its impact on Grandes Lignes earnings and the pressing issues of SNCF's long-term debt burden, justifying funds for TGV Est Éuropéen was by no means easy. At one stage SNCF's internal rate of return was 4.0% and the social-benefit rate was 9.4%, but these figures are now thought to be optimistic, although not low enough to prevent the go-ahead on a staged basis.

But the project – which is an 'aménagement du territoire' – does have very strong political support from the east of France, the only part of the country not served by a radial TGV from Paris. Compared with the two-hour rail journey from Paris to Lyon or Nantes and a three-hour journey from Paris to Bordeaux or London, the Paris – Strasbourg journey is four hours by classic train. Discussions are in progress between the French government, the regional authorities along the route and the EU on the basis that 20% of the traffic carried by this new TGV line would be international.

Given the lowish rate of return on an outlay of FFR 26.80 billion for the complete project, the French Government decided to phase its investment by giving the go-ahead for the first 270 or so kilometres from Vaires in the Ile-de-France to Vandières in the Moselle Valley. This was announced on 23 December 1996. The future of the rest of the project – from Vandières to the outskirts of Strasbourg – has been deferred, but could still go-ahead if funding can be organised under the aménagement due territoire procedures. One of the factors influencing the Government's decision is the possible use of a 350 km/h New Generation tilting TGV; with higher speeds possible over the first stage of the route and by utilising tilt technology on the classic tracks between Nancy and Strasbourg, a 2 hours 30 minutes journey-time between Paris and Strasbourg could be possible. Although this falls short of the 1 hour 50 minutes journey-time if the entire project is built, it is 90 minutes quicker than the existing classic train. This should enable SNCF to gain significant market share from air. Given that most of the towns on the first stage of the route – Reims, Nancy, Metz and Luxembourg – will obtain maximum journey-time benefits and that the project will include a link with the Jonction TGV line enabling through TGVs from other parts of France to access TGV Est Éuropéen, the rate of return for Stage 1 now justifies the go-ahead.

From its start at a high-speed grade-separated junction on the classic Paris – Strasbourg line, TGV Est Éuropéen initially heads north-east for 10 kilometres to a point where it crosses the north-south Paris interconnexion TGV line – La Jonction – approximately half way between Aéroport Charles-de-Gaulle and Marne-la-Vallée TGV stations. Here there will be two pairs of grade-separated junctions – from the Charles-de-Gaulle direction towards Strasbourg and from Marne-la-Vallée towards Strasbourg. From a point near Château-Thierry the railway runs alongside or quite close to the A4 autoroute to a point east of the city of Reims. There is to be a TGV railhead station – Gare Champagne Ardenne – at Bezannes just outside the south-west side of Reims, 113 kilometres (70 miles) from the start of the new line. Just beyond the station platforms – close to the village of Trois-Puits – is a 170 km/h grade-separated junction with the classic line from Epernay; this will be used for a service to the existing station in the centre of Reims, continuing thence to Charleville Mézières.

At St-Hilaire-au-Temple – 30 or so kilometres from Gare Champagne-Ardenne – there is a grade-separated connection with the Reims-Châlons-en-Champagne branch line. This will be the route for TGVs from Paris to key towns on the classic Paris Est-Strasbourg line – Châlons-en-Champagne, Vitry-le-François and Bar-le-Duc. This connection will also provide an emergency diversionary route. From St-Hilaire-au-Temple TGV Est Éuropéen continues towards a second TGV railhead station – Gare Meuse (Km 213) – to serve the nearby historic town of Verdun and Bar-le-Duc.

The end of TGV Est Éuropéen Stage 1 is Km 268 where there is to be a complicated series of junctions comprising north chords which take TGVs towards Metz joining the classic line at Pagny and south chords which take TGVs from Nancy joining/leaving the classic line at Vandières. While TGVs can reach or enter the high-speed line at 170 km/h, space precludes higher speeds to/from Pagny and Vandières. The north chord is the route to Metz, Thionville, Luxembourg; and the south chord is to Nancy, Epinal, Remiremont, Lunéville and St Dié.

TGV Est Éuropéen second stage – 93 kilometres from Prény to Réding – has three important features, the first of which is Gare Lorraine (Km 268) near Louvigny located 27 kilometres south of Metz and 36 kilometres north of Nancy. Gare Lorraine will provide regional links with Paris Airport (Roissy), Lille, Marne-la-Vallée (for Disneyland Paris), Massy, Rennes, Nantes and Bordeaux; the station would also have international services to Frankfurt. Eighteen kilometres beyond Gare Lorraine are further connections with the classic network, known as the Raccordements de Baudrecourt. The first starts at Km 298 and is a nine-kilometre single-chord joining the Metz – Sarrebruck line at Herny; this would be the route for TGVs from Paris to Frankfurt crossing into Germany at Forbach. The second connection – also a single-track chord – is from the Metz – Sarrebourg line joining TGV Est Éuropéen at Baudrecourt (Km 302) towards Strasbourg. Pending completion of the second stage, Paris – Strasbourg TGVs will use the classic network from Metz via Réding. This last segment through the Vosges mountains includes the 3.9-kilometre Saverne Tunnel (the only one on the route), after which the route is across the Alsace Plain.

As the line approaches the Strasbourg conurbation, provision has been made for a junction for a proposed branch passing to the north of the city of Strasbourg crossing the River Rhine to join the German network providing a route to Southern Germany and an alternative route through to Frankfurt.

The complete TGV Est Éuropéen ends at Vendenheim (km 407) where it joins the classic line from Paris Est some 10 kilometres from Strasbourg main station. As TGV Est Éuropéen will be laid out for standard SNCF left-hand running whereas the network in Alsace including Strasbourg station – which was originally built when Alsace was part of Germany – was laid out for and remains a right-hand running system, the track layout at Vendenheim includes some grade-separation and bi-directional signalling to Strasbourg station.

While the route for TGV Est Éuropéen has been defined in broad terms, a number of technical points of detail have yet to be settled. On present plans commercial services will be introduced at 300 km/h, but the design speed will be 350 km/h or possibly higher between Vaires and Vandières. Minimum radius curves will be 8,333 metres between Vaires and the Moselle area, allowing speeds higher than 350 km/h, and 7,143 metres over the eastern part of the route, giving a maximum speed of 350 km/h; there will be some exceptions to suit local conditions. Depending again on the maximum design speed, the space between track centres will be between 4.5 and 4.8 metres. Maximum gradient – limited to a distance of 6,500 metres (4 miles) – will be 3.5%. Power supplies will be 25 kV ac. Since all of northern and eastern France is already wired for 25 kV ac there will be no direct interface with 1.5 kV dc, although this voltage is necessary for inter-regional TGVs using the Grande Ceinture line en route to Massy for the Atlantique line. A different power supply – 15 kV $16^2/_3$Hz – will be necessary for cross-frontier working into Germany or Switzerland. The route will be signalled for full reversible working; the type of cab-signalling has not yet been decided, but the route could be the first to use the European Train Control System (ETCS).

Associated works

A comprehensive programme of essential works and modifications to existing classic routes will be necessary both to cope with the significant increase in train movements, and to provide easy access for TGVs to reach important destinations away from the core route.

Paris Est – Vaires-sur-Marne: To cope with the new levels of business and to maximise trainset utilisation, the train service plan will be based on in-and-out working with short turnrounds at Paris Est. This will entail some modifications to the existing platforms, the layout of the station throat and approach tracks. Additional tracks will be laid and grade-separations installed to facilitate the flow of traffic. Further out the line speed beyond Chenay-Gagny will be raised to 220 km/h to give fast access to the new line at Vaires-sur-Marne.

Electrification: The marketing strategy is to provide a TGV service to the maximum number of towns located on connecting branches. For TGVs to reach Châlons-en-Champagne, Vitry-le-François and Bar-le-Duc, 16 kilometres of route between St-Hilaire-au-Temple and Châlons-en-Champagne will be electrified. For TGVs to serve Epinal, Remiremont and Saint-Dié, three local lines in the Vosges region will be electrified. They are: Blainville – Epinal – Arches, 63 kilometres of double-track; Arches – Remiremont, 15 kilometres of single-track; and Lunéville – Saint-Dié, 51 kilometres of single-track. Associated work will include modifications to signalling and track layouts.

Terminating stations: Track alterations and platform lengthening will be necessary at Reims, Charleville-Mézières, Châlons-en-Champagne and Vitry-le-François. Similarly, siding and servicing facilities for TGVs will be necessary at Metz and Nancy.

Metz – Luxembourg: Following an accord between the French and Luxembourg governments, plans are being developed for the modernisation of the line between Metz and Luxembourg, including line speed and other improvements. This will be the route for a Paris – Luxembourg TGV service.

Strasbourg area: Given the superior acceleration and braking characteristics of TGV trainsets, the line speed over the 10 kilometres of route from the end of TGV Est Européen at Vendenheim to Strasbourg station will be raised from 160 to 220 km/h. With TGV services – both radial from Paris and inter-regional from other parts of France – studies show that the station area of Strasbourg is likely to become saturated. To minimise standing time in the station platforms and reduce the number of shunting movements by classic trains with separate locomotives, new stabling facilities are being developed so that trains can arrive into the station already cleaned and with their locomotive attached.

Strasbourg – Kehl: Until the high-speed link bypassing Strasbourg to the north of the city, where it will cross the River Rhine into Germany, is built, train services between France and Germany – TGVs or ICEs – will use the existing 8 kilometres of route from Strasbourg station to the River Rhine crossing the frontier at Kehl. On the French side, the Strasbourg – Kehl section will be upgraded to 160 km/h. On the German side of the Rhine, DB AG is implementing a major upgrade of its north to south main line with dedicated track for high-speed trains with 200 km/h or even higher speeds.

In this first-phase scenario, full TGV journey time benefits will be achieved over the western section of the project, including the major centres at Metz and Nancy plus Luxembourg. From Vandières the quickest route for Paris – Strasbourg TGVs is the Nancy – Metz line to a point south of Metz station, thence over the connecting lines from Metz through Réding and Saverne to Vendenheim. There will be a service of inter-réseau TGVs from Bordeaux, Rennes, Nantes and Lille to stations in Lorraine and Alsace. There will be a significant increase in the number of international services between Paris and Frankfurt – a 4-hour journey with six daily services. An interesting development would be an entirely new route to serve Basel and other points in Switzerland. Four daily TGVs will run beyond Strasbourg through Colmar and Mulhouse to Basel with extensions to Zürich. The Strasbourg – Basel line has already been upgraded to 200 km/h and a further improvement to 220 km/h is a possibility.

Trainsets

When the DUP submission was being prepared, the rolling stock requirement costed at 6,500 million francs was based on 68 trainsets – 42 SNCF Réseau and 26 international sets of which some would be provided (or funded) by SNCF's international partners. Things have now changed. SNCF and GEC Alsthom have now launched a project for a four-voltage 'New Generation' power car and the possibility of a tilting TGV is now being studied. It does not appear likely that the Réseau type will be perpetuated for TGV Est Éuropéen. A version of DB AG's ICE train is also a possibility, certainly for services to Germany. Maintenance of TGV Est Éuropéen trainsets will be at a new depot complex near Paris Est – routine maintenance will be at Ourcq and heavier maintenance at a purpose-built installation at Noisy-le-Sec.

JOURNEY TIME AND FREQUENCIES FROM PARIS

	Present Times		First Phase Times		Service	Second Phase Times		Service
Destination	Hr	Min	Hr	Min	TGVs/day	Hr	Min	TGVs/day
Reims	1	25	0	45	7	0	45	7
Charleville	2	23	1	30	2	1	30	2
Châlons-en-Champagne	1	21	0	55	2	0	55	2
Vitry-le-Fraçois	1	41	1	15	2	1	15	2
Bar-le-Duc	1	58	1	40	2	1	40	2
Metz	2	43	1	30	8	1	30	8
Luxembourg	3	32	2	15	4	2	15	4
Sarrebruck	3	40	2	20	3	1	50	3
Mannheim	5	03	3	20	6	2	50	6
Frankfurt	5	59	4	00	6	3	30	6
Nancy	2	39	1	30	8	1	30	8
Remiremont	4	11	2	45	2	2	45	2
Lunéville	3	01	1	50	1	1	50	1
Strasbourg	3	56	2	30	15	1	50	15
Colmar	4	46	3	00	3	2	20	3
Mulhouse	4	11	3	20	6	2	40	6
Basel	4	40	3	40	4	3	00	4

CHANNEL TUNNEL RAIL LINK

After 10 or so years of indecision, Britain is to have its first purpose-built high-speed railway. The catalyst for this is of course the Channel Tunnel. It is a matter of history that, compared with the rail routes from London to the North, the West, Wales and Scotland, Kent is not well served. Conceived in the Victorian era, the rail network through South East London to Kent is characterised by numerous low-speed flat junctions, critical two-track sections, and permanent speed restrictions, although some of these constraints were eased when the two routes from Waterloo International to the coast were upgraded for Channel Tunnel traffic.

Given the significant increase in both passenger and freight traffic expected following completion of the Channel Tunnel, in July 1988 British Rail published a report on long-term route and terminal capacity for the new international trains using the Channel Tunnel and the expected growth of commuter traffic. This concluded that a major increase of rail capacity in Kent would be necessary by the end of the century. In fact, as described in Chapter 20, there is already a problem – for the volume of commuter traffic leaving London for Kent between 1630 and 1900 is such that only five Eurostar paths can be made available in a period when many international passengers wish to travel.

Following consultation, British Rail presented plans for a new high-speed railway from the London area through Kent to the Channel Tunnel; this was rejected on grounds of cost. In spring 1991 a modified version which retained the basic route through the North Downs but offered a choice of four route options into Central London was published. In October 1991 the government endorsed British Rail's choice of route across the North Downs but rejected the southerly approach through South East London in favour of a different alignment passing under the River Thames near Ebbsfleet to make an easterly approach to King's Cross, which was retained as the preferred location for the second London international terminal. The government's decision was based on its wish to regenerate the East Thames corridor, although the political sensitivity of conservative-held parliamentary seats in Kent, where there was opposition to the construction of a new railway, was also thought to be a factor.

To meet the government's wishes for private-sector participation, in July 1992 the various parties working on the rail link project were merged into a new BR agency company – Union Railways – combining public and private-sector staff. The team's remit covered safety, business strategies, environment, design, operations, planning and consultation. Another development was the government's wish that the new railway should also be capable of conveying freight traffic.

Hitherto, King's Cross was the preferred second international terminal, but by now circumstances had begun to change. The international terminal station was to have been part of a vast project comprising a sub-surface station for international trains, a revamped Thameslink 2000 service, and new high-speed commuter trains from Kent. Improvements to the existing King's Cross and St Pancras surface stations were also part of this ambitious project. A substantial contribution to the cost of the King's Cross-St Pancras project was to have been made by redevelopment of the large area of unused land to the north of the two stations, the value of which would be considerably enhanced by this new international and domestic transport interchange.

By the start of the 1990s it was becoming clear that earlier assumptions regarding the King's Cross redevelopment prospects would – in the light of the economic recession and its impact on property values – have to be revised. This source of funding was now uncertain. While the King's Cross-St Pancras redevelopment project would provide excellent interchange opportunities, it made very little difference to the existing St Pancras terminal where space was – and would continue to be – under-utilised. It was against this background that Union Railways began to study the possibility of using the St Pancras terminal train shed for international and Kent commuter trains coming into London by the Channel Tunnel Rail Link (CTRL). The outcome of these further studies was a proposal for a revised routeing in tunnel from the Barking area in East London, coming into the St Pancras area from the north instead of the east. This would considerably reduce the cost of the sub-surface station, although a new more modest Thameslink station would still be necessary. The new layout provides the same routeings with the exception of access between the CTRL and the East Coast Main Line which entails reversal in St Pancras.

In March 1994 the Government initiated a competition to find a private-sector partner to take over the Rail Link project. Four pre-qualified bidders submitted tenders in March 1995; three months later Eurorail and London & Continental were named as preferred bidders. The basis for the tender was that in return for building the Rail Link – for which the Government would make a financial contribution as the railway would also benefit Kent commuters – the successful bidder would take over free of debt those former BR assets created to provide the Eurostar service from London to Paris and Brussels, the use of which would provide cashflow towards the cost of and eventual operation of the line. These assets include 18 Eurostar trainsets, North Pole International train servicing depot and servicing facilities at Longsight (Manchester) and Polmadie (Glasgow); part of the European Night Services train fleet and seven locomotives; Waterloo and Ashford International stations, and the development lands in the King's Cross and Stratford areas.

Announced in March 1996, the winner of the competition to build the Channel Tunnel Rail Link – now costed at around £3 billion – was London & Continental, a consortium formed by eight companies as shown below with their percentage shareholding.

Arup	2%	Civil and structural design engineers.
Bechtel	18%	One of the world's largest engineering, construction and project management companies.
Halcrow	2%	Railway and tunnelling design engineers.
London Electricity	12%	Prime supplier and distributor of electricity in London.
National Express	17%	Coach and train operator.
Systra	14%	The consultancy subsidiary of SNCF, with unique experience of design and construction of TGV lines.
Virgin	17%	Owner of Virgin Rail, and companies in travel, leisure and ancillary business.
S G Warburg	18%	Investment bank.

London & Continental took over European Passenger Services and Union Rail in March 1996 and the Channel Tunnel Rail Link Act received the Royal Assent in December 1996. Public services were scheduled to come into operation in March 2003 but the less than smooth progress of the project seems likely to delay this.

Comprising 108 kilometres (67.7 miles) of route the CTRL starts from the east side – platforms 5 to 13 – in the modified St Pancras trainshed. Here the platforms have been increased in number and extended in length to accommodate Eurostar trains. The tracks from these nine platforms – six for international and three for domestic services – turn sharply eastward, rising up to the level of the North London Line to enter the London Tunnel just under 1fi miles (2 kilometres) from the station.

The track layout in the St Pancras area – is complicated. There is access from the international platforms to the westbound North London Line leading to Camden Road and the West Coast Main Line, and to the East Coast Main Line in the opposite direction. The relocated Thameslink station has two northbound routes – to the Midland Main Line and to the East Coast Main Line.

Artist's impression of the Channel Tunnel Rail Link near the River Thames road crossing. *Peter Green, GRA*

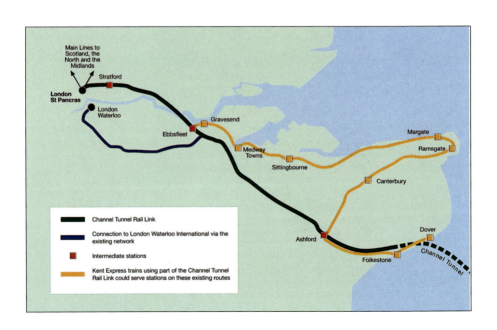

The aforementioned London Tunnel is twin-bore and extends for 12 miles (20 kilometres) to Ripple Lane to the east of Barking. At Stratford, half way along the tunnel, a major sub-surface international and domestic interchange between the Great Eastern, North London and Anglia surface lines; the Docklands Light Railway; and London Underground, Central and Jubilee Lines is planned. There will be an additional loop platform; access to a train servicing facility at nearby Temple Mills is also under study.

Emerging from the London Tunnel at Ripple Lane, 13 miles (21 kilometres) from St Pancras, the line is alongside the existing London Tilbury & Southend Railway; here there will be a connection with the existing railway and Ripple Lane freight yard. Continuing for 7½ miles (12 kilometres) along North Thameside the line changes direction near Aveley.

Beyond Aveley and near the Queen Elizabeth II Thames road bridge, the line enters the 2.8-kilometre twin-bore tunnels passing under the River Thames, emerging on the south-side at Ebbsfleet. Here a major Parkway station is planned. However, immediately before Ebbsfleet there is a junction leading to the North Kent Line toward Gravesend. This will be used by high-speed commuter trains from North Kent into London. Ebbsfleet main station layout has not yet been finalised, but one option is to have the non-stopping tracks on the outside with international and domestic platforms in the centre. There will also be platforms for the North Kent branch.

Immediately beyond Ebbsfleet at Kilometre 40 there is the Waterloo Connection. This junction leads to the disused Gravesend to Farningham Road trackbed which will be reinstated to provide access into London (Charing Cross, Victoria or Waterloo International) via Swanley. Unfortunately, as this route entails existing infrastructure with restricted line speeds, the journey time improvement for those Eurostars continuing to use Waterloo International will be less than the time gained by the new line into St Pancras.

Beyond Ebbsfleet the route is close to the A2/M2 roads passing to the south of Rochester and Chatham to the North Downs where there is a single-bore 3.2-kilometre (2-mile) tunnel, the north portal of which is 55 kilometres from St Pancras. South of North Downs Tunnel the alignment is north of Maidstone, thence alongside the M20 motorway to Ashford.

At Ashford the railway parts company with the A20 to pass through the town in cut-and-cover sections; at Godington Road Tunnel there are grade-separated junctions leading into and out of Ashford International station. East of the station the outbound track passes under the main tracks. For most of the final 15 kilometres from here to the Channel Tunnel the line is again alongside the M2 to Dollands Moor Freight Yard. Here the southbound (or outbound) track passes to the north of the yard with the northbound (or inbound) to the south to reach the interface with Eurotunnel, 108 kilometres from St Pancras, and 3 kilometres from the actual entry to the Tunnel.

Unlike the high-speed routes in France, the CTRL will be a multi-purpose railway for international trains, commuter trains, and is being designed to carry freight. Once clear of the St Pancras terminal area, the line speed will be 225 km/h (140 mph) as far as Ebbsfleet, including passage of the London Tunnel. With the exception of the Ashford area which will be 250/260 km/h, the line speed from Ebbsfleet to Dollands Moor will be 270 km/h (168 mph). Ruling gradient is 2.5% and the minimum curve radius will be 1,500 metres. Loading gauge will be UIC 'C' for freight trains between the Channel Tunnel Portal and Ripple Lane and UIC 'B' + for passage of the London Tunnels into St Pancras. This will allow normal European passenger stock – a TGV Duplex or a four-voltage PBKA THALYS trainset for example – to run through to St Pancras, subject of course to Channel Tunnel safety criteria. Maximum axle-loads will be 17 tonnes for passenger trains and 22 tonnes for freight trains which will be restricted to a maximum speed of 140 km/h (87 mph). The routes will be equipped with cab-signalling and Automatic Train Protection with a three-minute headway between trains in both directions. Two 2,000-metre freight loops – located at Singlewell and Lenham – will provide refuge for freight trains to be passed by faster trains. Power supplies will be 25 kV. During peak periods eight paths per hour will be provided for high-speed domestic commuter services.

THE NETHERLANDS SOUTH LINE

In November 1996 the Netherlands Parliament Upper Chamber approved the choice of route for a new high-speed line from Amsterdam to the Belgian border which will form part of the European high-speed network. The Netherlands South Line – which will be used by THALYS TGVs and Netherlands Railways (NS) domestic services – is one of two high-speed projects currently being developed. The second is the East Line from Amsterdam to the German border, although this is essentially an upgrading of the existing rail corridor rather than new 'greenfields' construction.

The case for the South Line – the cost of which is around 7.5 billion guilders – is not speed *per se* but is based on the need for additional rail infrastructure to increase capacity to meet the growing levels of passenger traffic which the Netherlands government is encouraging as the means of protecting the environment in this small and increasingly crowded country. During the past few years NS has undertaken significant investment in new railway infrastructure to eliminate bottlenecks and to open up new connections in the national network. A particular example is the new four-track tunnel under the Nieuwe Maas, to the south of Rotterdam Central station, eliminating the lifting bridge which was a long-standing impediment to efficient train working. The NS Rail 21 long-term investment strategy together with the South and East Lines is part of a nationally co-ordinated infrastructure programme including roads and expansion at Schiphol Airport. A fifth runway at Schiphol and the South Line are inter-dependent projects. As well as providing an important part of the European high-speed rail network, the South Line will greatly improve access between Amsterdam, Rotterdam, Den Haag (The Hague) – the three principal centres in the Randstad region – and Utrecht.

Given the Netherlands population density, the route for new infrastructure was bound to be controversial, even though the new sections of railway are relatively short. For the first 17 kilometres from Amsterdam Central station high-speed trains will use the existing suburban route through Sloterdijk and Lelylaan to reach the 5.8-kilometre Schiphol Tunnel. From Schiphol Airport station the route continues for 5.3 kilometres to Hoofddorp, where there will be a grade-separated junction leading to 48 kilometres of new high-speed infrastructure to the outskirts of Rotterdam. The new railway passes to the east of Leiden through the so-called 'Green Heart' of Holland. To protect this sensitive area, part of this section will be in a 9-kilometre twin-bore tunnel. After passing to the east of Zoetermeer, the line crosses the existing Utrecht – Den Haag line, before reaching a covered box section to protect Noordrand and Bergschenhoek. South Line trains will use classic tracks for the passage of the Rotterdam area including Central Station, accessed through a grade-separated junction on the Delft line. The distance from the start of the new infrastructure at Hoofddorp to Rotterdam is 48 kilometres.

From Rotterdam Central Station trains will follow the existing route to the south through the new Rotterdam Tunnel for a distance of 7 kilometres to the start of the south section of the route at Barendrecht, access to which is through a grade-separated junction. For the first few kilometres the line runs to the west of Dordrecht as far as Gravendeel, where the high-speed tracks then run alongside the classic line from Rotterdam to the south, crossing the wide Hollands Diep estuary on a new 1.3-kilometre bridge located alongside the existing structure. From here the new infrastructure parallels the Rotterdam to Breda line, before passing to the west of the city. However, there is to be a double connection so that trains from both the Rotterdam and Antwerp directions can join the classic tracks to provide a service into and out of the important town of Breda. After Breda the route follows the A16/E19 motorway to Hazeldonk until it crosses the Netherlands border to link up with the northwards extension of the Belgian line described in Chapter 7.

The distance from the start of the south section at Barendrecht to the Belgian frontier is 47.6 kilometres; the distance from the frontier to the point where the Belgian high-speed line joins the existing classic SNCB network is 35 kilometres; and from there the distance into Antwerp Central station is five kilometres.

Both sections of the new South Line will be engineered for a maximum speed of 300 km/h (186 mph). Minimum radius curves will be 2,500 metres and the maximum gradient will be 2.5%. Space between track centres will be 4.5 metres and the width of the track base will be 13.6 metres. Structures include 12.4 kilometres of twin-bore tunnels, 6.3 kilometres of cut-and-cover tunnelled sections, 14.5 kilometres of viaducts and, as mentioned, the 1.3-kilometre Hollands Diep bridge. All tunnel sections will have seven-metre height clearance and 70 square metres of free air space allowing speeds of 300 km/h. The route will be signalled for full bi-directional working; the type of cab-signalling system has not yet been decided, but the new European Train Control System is one of the options.

Although the Netherlands network is currently equipped with 1.5 kV dc power supplies, the South Line will be equipped for 25 kV ac. Given the significant increase in train movements during the past few years, NS now believes that a change to the more efficient 25 kV ac is inevitable and will have to be made sometime in the longer term, although the practicalities and cost of the changeover will be formidable.

Development of the South Line international passenger business is the responsibility of NV Hogesnelheidstrein (HST), a wholly-owned subsidiary of NS, which manages the Dutch end of the Paris-Brussels-Amsterdam (PBA) THALYS TGV service.

Completion of the Netherlands South Line and the Belgian lines will enable significant journey time reductions for international trains. When the next stage of the Belgian line (Antoing to the outskirts of Brussels Midi station) is commissioned in December 1997, journey times between Amsterdam Central and Paris Nord will be reduced from 4 hours 45 minutes to 4 hours 15 minutes. When the South Line is operational in 2005, HST envisage a service of 14 trains per day in each direction between Amsterdam Central and Paris Nord with a journey time of 3 hours 10 minutes. Depending on the completion date of the British Channel Tunnel Rail Link, a 4-hour service between Amsterdam and London may also be a possibility.

Another plan being developed by NS is for a new international terminal station on the Amsterdam South Ring Line close to the proposed World Trade Centre. A new connection is planned at Duivendrecht so that international trains from the Utrecht direction can reach the South Ring Line for the new international station and for a more direct route to Schiphol airport; THALYS trains will go direct from the South Line to the Amsterdam South Ring route. The new Amsterdam International station will relieve the ever increasing pressure on Amsterdam Central station and its approach tracks.

For domestic customers, NS is considering a service of four trains an hour between Amsterdam Central, Schiphol Airport and Rotterdam Central, with extensions to Breda. Journey time from Amsterdam Central to Rotterdam Central will be about 35 minutes compared with 60 minutes by today's fastest inter-city service; Amsterdam Central Station to Breda will be around 60 minutes and Schiphol Airport to Rotterdam around 19 minutes. These will be provided by dual-voltage high-speed trains operating with a maximum speed of 220 or even 300 km/h. One possibility is the purchase of a number of second-hand SNCF Paris Sud Est trainsets, should some be available. An international regional-type service between Antwerp Central and Breda is also an option under study in association with SNCB.

It is hoped that the line will be open for business in 2005.

TGVs FOR THE 21ST CENTURY

For 20 or so years SNCF and its partners in the railway manufacturing industry have been the leaders in the development of high-speed rail technology. In 1972 the experimental gas-turbine unit TGV 001 achieved a speed of 318 km/h (197.6 mph). Six years later, a pre-series PSE trainset achieved a speed of 260 km/h (161.5 mph) on the easily-graded line across the Alsace plain between Strasbourg and Colmar. On 26 February 1981, seven months before the opening of the first (southern) section of the new PSE line, Unit 16 achieved a speed of 380 km/h (236 mph). In December 1988, PSE Unit 88 – equipped with synchronous traction motors in a reduced formation – achieved a new world speed record of 408.4 km/h (253.8 mph). With the Atlantique line open, further tests were made with Atlantique Unit 325 and a new world speed record of 482.3 km/h (299.7 mph) was achieved on 5 December 1989. As this fell below the target speed, a further series of tests provided a new world speed record of 515.3 km/h (320.2 mph) on 18 May 1990 on the Aquitaine branch of the new Atlantique line. For these last two tests Unit 325 consisted of two power cars and only three trailers; weight was 258.8 tonnes and length 106.6 metres.

While a world speed record provides good publicity for the French railway industry, it is just one highlight in an on-going programme of serious research, the purpose of which is to pursue the limits of technology. Much has been achieved. Vehicle suspension systems have been upgraded to minimise track wear and improve ride quality; new pantographs have been developed to improve current collection from the overhead line at much higher speeds; braking has been improved; conventional traction motors have been replaced by the lighter and more efficient three-phase ac synchronous and asynchronous motors; and by using aluminium instead of stainless steel vehicle weights have been reduced. The validity of this research is best illustrated by comparing the basic details of the original PSE and the latest double-deck Duplex TGV.

The number of seats has been increased from 368 to 516, the power of the train has been raised from 6,450 to 8,800 kW, the number of traction motors has been reduced from 12 to 8, the mass of the train has been reduced from 385 to 380 tonnes, power-to-weight ratio has been increased from 22.46 to 31.04 hp per tonne – only the 200.19-metre length is the same – and the customer has a superior product. As well as being 15% more cost-effective than previous TGV designs, the latest braking systems and traction motors generate far less noise and minimise environmental disturbance. When the present order for 30 Duplex and 17 PBKA trainsets has been completed by the end of 1998, the present phase of TGV development will have been concluded, although options to increase the number of trains in these two orders are still in place.

Research and development is on-going. GEC Alsthom in close collaboration with SNCF is leading the development of a new range of trains built for the home and export market. There are three inter-related areas of development – the TGV Nouvelle Génération (TGV NG) power car, the application of tilting (or pendular) technology, and a range of vehicles which can be used to form trainset configurations to suit customer requirements.

TGV Nouvelle Génération: While 300 km/h is a routine feature of French rail travel, this is well below the upper limit of TGV speed potential. If higher speeds are to be achieved, a deeper knowledge of track geometry, current collection, bogie performance and vehicle design and their complex behaviour patterns at higher speeds is essential. To pursue this research GEC Alsthom and SNCF – with 535 million francs support from the French Government – are developing a new-generation TGV power car, TGV NG. This will be an inter-European, four-voltage unit with sufficient power and speed to meet journey-time aspirations of 1,000 kilometres (621 miles) to be covered in 3 hours – a *vitesse commerciale* of 330 km/h (207 mph). In its contract with GEC Alsthom SNCF had already ordered a spare Duplex power car and this will instead be built as the prototype NG vehicle. Due for completion at Belfort in summer 1998, the NG power car will be tested with a Réseau or PBKA eight-car rake; in 1999 it will be tested in Germany.

Experience gained from these tests will be incorporated in a new double-deck train using the standard two power car eight articulated trailer format. Technical features will include:

Traction motors Given that an increase in speed from 300 to 360 km/h necessitates a 50% increase in electric power, the NG will need six motor bogies, each with two traction motors rated between 1,200 to 1,250 kW, giving a total of 15,000 kW per trainset. As with the PSE and Eurostar configurations, one motor bogie will be positioned at either end of the eight-car rake under R1 and R8. Like Eurostar, the NG will be equipped with asynchronous motors giving an outstanding weight/power ratio of one kilogram per kilowatt.

Control pantographs A universal design pantograph to facilitate current capture above 300 km/h and allow trains to run throughout Europe.

Comfort and stability To reduce vibration and optimise passenger comfort, researchers are studying bogies, track, and wheel-rail interaction.

Braking As adhesion braking has an upper limit of around 320 km/h, for higher speeds eddy currents have opened the way to a braking system that avoids conventional reliance on wheel-rail contact.

Noise reduction By optimising wheel, track, and rail grinding, running can be reduced by 5 dB – but only on condition that aerodynamic noises are also reduced. Here one solution is to streamline all sources of aerodynamic turbulence.

Lighter coaches Following successful application in Formula 1 motor racing and aeronautics, composite materials could soon be used in trains. The aim is to reduce coach weight by 30%, with consequent reductions of energy and gains in speed.

Tilting TGVs: Following the Rouvillois Report (Chapter 24) but also because the benefits of tilting trains have now gained worldwide acceptance, GEC Alsthom and SNCF are studying pendular technology for use in its next generation of TGV and classic trains.

When any vehicle runs through a curve a centrifugal force is created which seeks to send the vehicle off at a tangent – literally – to the curve. In the case of a railway, the outer rail on curved track must be raised to counteract this centrifugal force, in order to avoid excessive forces on the track (with consequent high maintenance costs) and passenger discomfort. But there is a practical limit on how much superelevation, or cant, may be applied. Most European railways set this limit at 150 mm (alternatively expressed as 6°).

As cant is proportional to the square of the speed and inversely proportional to the radius of the curve, tighter curves need more cant for a given speed. If the amount of cant exceeds the amount a railway allows, then a speed restriction below the line-limit must be imposed. Since the acceptable speed is set by passenger comfort rather than by the far higher level at which derailment might occur, it is possible to raise speeds significantly over a curving railway by tilting the coach bodies themselves inwards to provide additional curve compensation for the passengers. Such tilt can be passive (when the coach body simply swings, as it were) or active (when the tilt is brought about by hydraulic or electrical means). While some outlay will be necessary to modify the signalling system for higher speeds, and perhaps for some civil engineering too, worthwhile journey-time reductions can be obtained without the need for costly track realignment projects or the construction

Artist's impression of a new generation TGV power car. *SNCF*

of new infrastructure. Tilting trains now run successfully in Sweden, Germany, Switzerland, Italy, Spain, and other countries; tilt is now the chosen technology for the AMTRAK 'American Flyer' and for the British West Coast main line.

There were other factors. Given the very high quality of its infrastructure, SNCF has been able to work with a maximum cant of 7.25° and a similar maximum cant deficiency (180 mm in both cases) rather than the 6° figures used elsewhere, and this means that it has less to gain from tilt than its European neighbours.

Both the old British Rail and SNCF considered pendular suspension in the 1970s. The British pursued the project for several years but – lacking Government funds and commitment – gave up the project. According to some of the engineers involved, a few more months and a little more cash would have bought the concept to a successful conclusion, enabling proper commercial development. SNCF considered tilt in the late 1960s and its 1969 build of 'Grand Confort' TEE coaches were designed with this in mind. Following tests the concept was not pursued. By this time SNCF was moving to a high-speed strategy with new purpose-built lines with trains able to run at speeds between 250–300 km/h. These new lines would also provide a significant capacity enhancement and provide relief to the existing classic lines which would be able to handle more medium-distance passenger trains and slow-moving freight trains.

Type of Train	Track Characteristics: Permitted Speeds		
	Curve Radius 350 metres	Curve Radius 600 metres	Curve Radius 1,000 metres
Classic train with Italian, German and Swedish passenger comfort standards	95km/h	125km/h	160km/h
Classic train with French passenger comfort standards	100km/h	130km/h	170km/h
Tilting trains with European track resistant regulations	110km/h	145km/h	190km/h

To evaluate tilting-train potential in France, SNCF is to equip two types of stock with experimental pendular suspension. In June 1997, a Paris Sud Est first class trainset, surplus to operational requirements, was withdrawn so that the eight-car rake, but not the power cars, could be equipped with pendular suspension. This train – which will be reduced to six trailers – is to be tested at speeds up to 220 km/h on classic routes and 320 km/h on TGV lines. Later in 1997, following an agreement between SNCF and Fiat to study a new air-suspension pendular bogie devised from those in use on the ETR 460 Pendolino train, one of the new X 72500 diesel multiple unit trains is to be equipped with a new experimental Fiat bogie.

Tilting trains are now a political issue in France. Concerned that they may not now have new TGV lines, some of the French *régions* have expressed keen interest in tilting trains. Under an agreement signed in October 1996, using the *Aménagement et au Développement du Territoire* procedures, the French Government, SNCF and, the Conseils Régionaux du Centre, du Limousin and Midi-Pyrénées, signed a convention to fund the study of tilting train technology for the Paris Austerlitz – Orléans – Limoges – Brive – Toulouse classic line. To evaluate engineering parameters – including track, catenary, quality of ride – and the feasibility of journey-time reductions between Paris Austerlitz and Limoges, SNCF used an Italian ETR 460 for a series of test runs in February and March 1997. As well as using the results of its studies conducted in the 1960s and 1970s, GEC Alsthom is involved with other rail manufacturers. A particular example is the AMTRAK North East corridor project where the 'American Flyer' train has been developed using GEC Alsthom's TGV technology in partnership with Bombardier's tilt technology.

Mini TGVs

With the exception of Eurostar where special circumstances apply, most TGV trainsets have capacities ranging from 360 to 545 seats in the Duplex. While these are suitable for busy routes such as Paris-Lyon, there are many secondary destinations where shorter trains would be more cost-effective. Another issue is that, by the end of the 1990s, the early vehicles in the large fleet of over 3,000 Corail locomotive-hauled coaches which entered service from the mid-1970s will be life-expired and due for replacement. By this time TGV Méditerranée will be complete, giving an opportunity to restructure of the network of classic Corail multi-portion cross-country trains on journeys such as Metz–Nice, Geneva–Nice, Geneva–Perpignon, Lyon–Narbonne, Strasbourg–Nice and Strasbourg–Port Bou. If these classic trains are replaced by TGV-style equipment, the service could be transferred to the high-speed network from Lyon to Montpellier and Marseille with significant journey-time benefits, which would do much to rejuvenate this market. The type of train SNCF has in mind for this market is the Mini-TGV. Two versions are being studied – a single-deck with 169 to 179 seats or a double-deck with 235 seats. Each type will have a power car plus four articulated trailers; the end vehicle would include a driving cab. One, two, three or four trains could be joined together to run in multiple as a four, eight, 12 or 16-car rake. Multiple unit trains can couple/uncouple more quickly than conventional material and fewer locomotives will be required.

TGV: A WORLD PRODUCT

Thanks to on-going national and regional funding support for rail and metro projects, France is a world leader in train building and rail technology. Supported by this strong home market, France is well established as a major exporter of railway equipment and source of expertise, particularly for the less-developed areas in the world economy.

The leader in this field is the SYSTRA Group, with a 72% shareholding held equally by SNCF and RATP (Paris Transport Authority) and 28% held by various French banks. There are five divisions within the group, the largest of which is SYSTRA SOFRETU-SOFERAIL. SOFRETU deals with urban transport, buses, people-movers, tramways, light rail, urban railways, automatic guided transits, subway systems and mass transit rail. SOFERAIL deals with 'heavy' rail – bulk transport, industrial product transport in special-purpose wagons, container transport, unit trains, mail and package transportation, multimodal transport, urban and suburban trains, long-distance classic passenger trains and high-speed rail systems.

This corporate structure ensures that the SYSTRA companies are independent of any individual manufacturer or supplier of equipment. SOFERAIL offers a range of services, all of which are related to rail expertise or technology – operating, marketing and design, technical assistance and training. The company has a permanent staff of about 300 which is strengthened from time-to-time on an ad-hoc basis by experts and specialists from SNCF who undertake specific short-term assignments. Typically, 80,000 work-hours per year are undertaken in SNCF design offices.

TGV has generated world-wide interest. Because there are or will be direct links between the SNCF network and neighbouring railways in Belgium, Britain, Germany, Switzerland and Spain, TGV technology has been used for cross-frontier services such as Eurostar and THALYS. Although the Spanish AVE is for the present a self-contained system, the choice of basic GEC Alsthom technology for the trains is significant. GEC Alsthom has been involved in all of these developments and SYSTRA expertise has been sought for a number of support and related projects.

South Korea

The first TGV project outside Europe to receive the go-ahead is the 432-kilometre (268-mile) purpose-built high-speed line from the capital of South Korea, Seoul, through Cheonan, Daejeon, Daegu, Kyeongju to Pusan.

Initial studies started in 1982, but a government decision was not made until 1991 when the Korean High Speed Rail Corporation (KHRC) invited Mitsubishi, Siemens and GEC Alsthom to tender for the supply of rolling stock, catenary and signalling systems together with transfer of technology and financing proposals. Because bidding for the contract was so keen, negotiations continued for two years, when the TGV Korean Consortium (which is led by GEC Alsthom) won the contract in August 1993. The Consortium's Korean partners – Hyundai, Daewoo and Hanjin industries – will receive full transfer of technology.

The US $2.1 billion contract, of which the local manufacturing content is 50%, covers:

A fleet of 46 TGV trainsets, 34 of which will be built in Korea. Hyundai will test and assemble the trains; Daewoo will supply the power cars; Hanjin will manufacture the powered coaches.

Cegelec, an Alcatel Alsthom subsidiary, will supply the overhead line equipment.

CS Transport will install TVM 430 cab-signalling.

SOFERAIL will provide training for train operating and maintenance staff.

On 29 May 1997 GEC Alsthom presented its first completed pre-series TGV trainset to the Korean High Speed Rail Authority at its Aytré, La Rochelle, factory. This first train will undergo a 20-month test programme on SNCF high-speed tracks; the second pre-series set has been shipped out to Korea. Series construction will commence with 10 trainsets in France followed by the 34 remaining trainsets which will be built in Korea. Note the strong family resemblance with the trainsets built for France. *GEC Alsthom*

Due to enter service in 2000 with 69 million passengers per year, carryings are expected to grow to 122 million by 2010. To cope with these traffic volumes, KHRC has chosen a 20-vehicle trainset configuration, similar in concept to Eurostar. Formation will consist of two half-sets. The first half includes power car with five second class and four first class trailers; the other half consists of nine second class trailers plus a power car. Each set has six motor bogies – two under each power car and one under each of the outer ends of R1 and R18.

The project will open in two stages – the first section from Seoul to Daejon in 2000 followed by Daejon to Pusan at the end of 2001. South Korea is the first Asian country to launch a rail project using European-style 300 km/h high-speed trains.

TGV Korea second class interior. *GEC Alsthom*

Korean TGV first class interior; note roof-mounted video screen. *GEC Alsthom*

United States

Although jet aircraft ended the great era of the American transcontinental train, when you could travel the 2,500 miles from New York City to Los Angeles in superb luxury, there are still parts of the United States where the market can support a European-style high-speed rail service. The prime example is the AMTRAK North East Corridor route from Washington DC to New York City and thence to New Haven and Boston. As discussed later, the centre-to-centre journey time between Washington DC and New York City is under three hours for the 240-mile journey, which compares favourably with a parallel air route, but without the hassle.

There are other parts of the United States where the distribution of population and industry is such that journey times of up to three hours' duration by inter-city trains can be a viable alternative to air or road transport. Some states are now becoming concerned about congested roads and the cost of building new highways; air space is also becoming congested and the cost of expanding airports or even new airport construction is generally prohibitive. Impressed by developments in Europe and Japan, many cities are now subsidising mass transit systems; this philosophy may also be appropriate for high-speed inter-city rail.

Texas Super Train

Impressed by TGV in France, a group of Texas businessmen saw the potential for a high-speed rail link which could solve the growing problems of air and road traffic congestion with the Texas triangle formed by the Dallas-Fort Worth in the North, San Antonio in the South West and Houston in the South East. Following a SOFERAIL feasibility study in 1984 a group – known as the Texas Super Train Consortium – was formed by Morrison Knudsen and GEC Alsthom Bombardier to develop the 880-kilometre (547-mile) network. SOFERAIL was also involved in the project. In 1994 the consortium was awarded the franchise to design, build and operate the new high-speed line, the cost of which was around $6.8 billion, but with the proviso that the project would be privately-funded and there would be no state or federal financial support. Unfortunately, the consortium was unable to kindle sufficient financial interest to proceed with the project. Whether or not another group will be able to proceed at a later date remains to be seen.

Florida Overland Express (FOX)

Florida has been much more successful. Concerned again about road and air space congestion, in 1984 the State of Florida commissioned a preliminary SOFERAIL feasibility study for a TGV line from Miami on the south-east Atlantic coast of the state, running north through West Palm Beach to Orlando and thence heading south back down to Tampa in the Gulf of Mexico side of the state. Initially, it took some time for the project to gain momentum, but it was revived in May 1992. The successful bidder is a consortium known as the Florida Overland Express (FOX) formed by four key companies – Fluor Daniel, Odebrecht, GEC Alsthom and Bombardier. Fluor Daniel is the USA's largest publicly-traded engineering and construction company and Odebrecht is a specialist in large engineering project management. In addition, FOX has engaged SOFERAIL to act as consultant in preparing its operations.

FOX – the cost of which is $5 billion – is a joint-venture between private business and the State of Florida. As well as taking up to $58 million of FOX equity and guarantees of up to $290 million, the state will also contribute a subsidy of $70 million a year for the duration of the 40-year concession. This significant use of public funds is in recognition of the social-cost benefits which the project will generate in particular a reduction of investment in road and airport infrastructure.

FOX services will be provided by a fleet of 21 state-of-the-art trainsets formed with eight articulated coaches enclosed by two power cars. Passenger capacity is 295 seats. Power output is 8,000 kW (under 25 kV catenary), providing a normal operating speed of 320 km/h

(200 mph). Interior fittings will include telephone, fax and photocopy facilities, modem plugs and an electronic passenger information system and a catering facility. Initially, departures will be every 30 minutes during peak periods and hourly at other times of the day. Journey time from Tampa to Orlando International Airport – with stops at Lakeland and Orlando Attractions – is 60 minutes. Non-stop journey time from Orlando International Airport to Miami is 1 hour 25 minutes. Services on the south-eastern leg of the network from Orlando International Airport to Miami will include intermediate stops at West Palm Beach and West Broward. Construction of the Miami – Orlando section is expected to start in October 1999 with launch of public services in April 2003; work on the Orlando – Tampa section will start in October 2001 with launch of services in June 2005.

FOX is a watershed in American public transport policy and could well be a catalyst for the revival of the Texas Super Train and other projects such as Los Angeles – Las Vegas (360 kilometres) and Los Angeles – San Francisco (600 kilometres) which have also been the subject of SOFERAIL feasibility studies.

The American Flyer

An interesting feature of the FOX project is the collaboration between GEC Alsthom and the Canadian train building company Bombardier. Bombardier is well established in North American markets, particularly in urban and metro train building, and a link up with GEC Alsthom to develop high-speed rail is good for both parties. Bombardier has also developed its own tilting system.

To develop high-speed rail in North America, the companies have devised a new product – known as the American Flyer – incorporating GEC Alsthom TGV technology with Bombardier tilt systems. The first fruits of this collaboration are the successful bid to supply new trains for the upgrading of the Washington DC – New York City – Boston AMTRAK North East Corridor service classic service referred to earlier. Although the Swedish X2000 and Siemens' Inter City Express (ICE) trainsets were shipped to the United States for in-service technical and passenger evaluation trials between Washington and New York, AMTRAK eventually chose the American Flyer. This is the first high-speed order to be placed in the United States.

Although the American Flyer incorporates TGV technology, the locomotives and coaches are based on classic individual coaches and the articulated format favoured for TGV has not been used. Each American Flyer AMTRAK trainset will consist of two power cars and six 26-metre non-articulated trailers. The two four-axle power cars have a rating of 4,600 kW (9,200 kW for the complete trainset) and are equipped with four asynchronous traction motors; two GTO (gate turn off) traction inverters will be used. Maximum speed is 150 mph. Power cars will be equipped with state-of-the-art monitoring and diagnostic equipment, and can operate with the two older AMTRAK ac power supply systems – 12.5 kV 60 Hz and 12 kV 25 Hz – plus 25 kV 60 Hz for the New Haven – Boston electrification, the execution of which is part of the general upgrading project. Trainset length is 200 metres. Given the combination of a conventional rather than an articulated configuration (12 instead of 7 bogies), Federal Railroad Administration (FRA) crashworthiness criteria, and stainless steel bodies, the weight of the train is 550 tonnes. Axle load is 22 tonnes. Power-to-weight ratio is 22.4 hp per tonne compared with 30.8 hp for a Réseau TGV.

GEC Alsthom will design the power cars and the locomotives and will supply the traction equipment, electric and electronic components, and the powered and non-powered bogies. Manufacture began at the end of 1997. The coaches, power cars and locomotives are being built at Bombardier's factory in Canada. Assembly of the coaches will be carried out at Barré, Vermont, and of the power cars and locomotives at Plattsburg, New York. The contract also covers the building of fully-equipped maintenance centres at Washington, New York and Boston. The North East Corridor project is essentially an upgrade and the trains will be formed with power cars with classic tilting coaches, so they are not strictly TGV trains, but they do include a significant content of TGV technology.

Unlike other trains in the TGV family, the AMTRAK American Flyer consists of separate power cars and non-articulated tilting coaches. *Artist's impression: Bombardier GEC Alsthom*

Amtrak: American Flyer	
Number of trainsets	18
Formation:	Two power cars plus six tilting coaches
Length	200.3 metres
Seats	301
Mass: empty	550 tonnes
Maximum service speed	240km/h: 150 mph
Power Car traction package	4 x 1,150 kW asyncronous motors = 4.600 kW (6.166hp)
Power supply	12.5 kV ac for existing routes 25 kV ac for New Haven-Boston

Interior view of AMTRAK's American Flyer. Only one class of seating is planned for this. *Bombardier GEC Alsthom*

Taiwan

Although outline plans for the Taipei – Kaohsiung high-speed rail link are well advanced, the decision has taken several years to mature. A joint venture with GEC Alsthom and Siemens has been selected by the Taiwan High Speed Rail Corporation (THSRC) as 'best applicant' in the bidding to build the new railway. SOFERAIL was engaged to undertake preliminary planning studies, although the building of the line and the supply of the trains could awarded either to France, Germany or Japan. The length of the line is 350 kilometres (217 miles) and the maximum speed is expected to be 350 km/h. Between 60 and 70 million passengers per year are expected to use the system. Estimated cost is around $15 billion.

Australia

Between 1986 and 1990 SOFERAIL undertook a series of studies into the feasibility and economics of an 876-kilometre (544-mile) high-speed line linking Sydney, Canberra and Melbourne. Subsequently, a private-venture company – formed by Speedrail Pty and GEC Alsthom Australia – was formed to develop the first stage from Sydney to Canberra. The Canberra – Sydney section is a long-term aspiration. Speedrail's route will involve some 50 kilometres of existing railway in the Sydney and Canberra suburban areas and approximately 270 kilometres (168 miles) of new purpose-built high-speed infrastructure. There will be stations at Mascot Airport, Southern Highlands and Goulburn. Much of the route will be built alongside or very close to existing motorways. Initial operating speed will be 300 km/h, although the line and the trains will be designed for a potential of 350 km/h. Journey time from Sydney to Canberra will probably be around 80 minutes. Work could start around 2000.

Canada

The Canadian High Speed Train project was established in February 1990 when Bombardier announced its decision to promote the construction of a high-speed railway between Quebec and Ontario, within the framework of an agreement with GEC Alsthom for the development of TGV in North America. Quebec, Montreal, Ottawa, Toronto and Windsor will be served by a 1,215-kilometre (750-mile) rail link with operating speeds at 300 km/h. SOFERAIL have been involved in preliminary technical and economic feasibility studies. The operator of these high-speed services has not yet been decided. Traffic potential is 10 million passengers per year. Trainsets will carry 366 passengers and will be formed with two power cars and eight trailers.

Russia

With the need to relieve pressure on the existing rail network between Moscow and Saint Petersburg, the Russian Government has initiated studies into a new high-speed rail link between the two cities. Following the signing of a decree by Boris Yeltsin, the President of Russia, a Russian company – High Speed Mainline Railways – has been created to develop the construction of a new railway between Saint Petersburg and Moscow and the acquisition of rolling stock, including inter-city high speed and commuter trains. Long distance passenger traffic between the two cities and the intermediate stations will be transferred to the new railway, releasing capacity on the existing network for the more efficient transport of freight traffic. The new company has engaged SOFERAIL for economic and feasibility studies. The 654-kilometre (406-mile) railway will be operated by a fleet of 30 high-speed trains consisting of two power cars and 12 trailers, with an operating speed of 300 km/h. A service of 30 trains per day in each direction is envisaged by the year 2005, but at the time of writing no invitation to tender had been issued.

TGV TRAINSETS: BASIC DETAILS

	PSE	Atlantique	Réseau	Eurostar Capitals	Eurostar Regional	Duplex	PBKA	AVE	Korea
Configuration	PC+8T+PC	PC+10T+PC	PC+8T+PC	PC+18T+PC	PC+14T+PC	PC+8T+PC	PC+8T+PC	PC+8T+PC	PC+18T+PC
Train length	200,190 m	237,590 m	200,190 m	393,720 m	318,920 m	200,190 m	200,190 m	200,190 m	388,000 m
Vehicle width	2,814 m	2,904 m	2,904 m	2,814 m	2,814 m	2,896 m	2,904 m	2,904 m	2,904 m
Power car bogie spacing	14,000 m	14,000 m	14,000 m	14,000 m	14,000 m	14,000 m	14,000 m	14,000 m	14,000 m
Coach length	18,700 m	18,700 m	18,000 m	18,700 m	18,700 m	18,700 m	18,700 m	18,700 m	18,700 m
Bogie length	3,000 m	3,000 m	3,000 m	3,000 m	3,000 m	3,000 m	3,000 m	3,000 m	3,000 m
Number of carrying bogies	7	11	9	18	14	9	9	9	18
Wheel diameter	920 m	920 m	920 m	920 m	920 m	920 m	920 m	920 m	920 m
Mass: net	385,000 kg	444,000 kg	383,000 kg	752,400 kg	665,000 kg	380,000 kg	385,000 kg	393,000 kg	698,800 kg
Mass: gross	418,000 kg	484,000 kg	416,000 kg	816,000 kg	680,000 kg	424,000 kg	424,000 kg	416,000 kg	773,800 kg
Maximum Speed	270 km/h	300 km/h	300 km/h	300 km/h	300 km/h	300 km/h	300 km/h	300 km/h	300 km/h
Traction motor power	537 kW	1100 kW	1100 kW	1020 kW	1020 kW	1100 kW	1100 kW	1100 kW	1100 kW
Number of traction motors	12	8	8	12	12	8	8	8	12
Number of motor bogies	6	4	4	6	6	4	4	4	6
Total Power: kW	6450	8800	8800	12200	12200	8800	8800	8800	13200
Total power: HP	8,646	11,796	11,796	16,354	16,354	11,796	11,796	11,796	17,694
Power: weight ratio HP/Tonne	22.46	26.56	30.79	21.74	24.59	31.04	30.64	30.02	25.32
Total seats	368	485	377	770	558	516	377	329	935